Praise for *The Blitz*

One of the brightest female leaders of her generation, Tamar shares her remarkable journey from a young woman navigating the chaos of a nation, in transition to becoming a leader who reshaped Georgia's financial landscape while facing and overcoming profound personal struggles. Her story is a testament to the strength, courage, and determination of Georgian women and serves as an inspiring example for anyone seeking to navigate their own life's challenges. Tamar empowers other women to embrace their potential, face their fears, and overcome obstacles, no matter how insurmountable they may seem.

—Kakha Shengelia
President of Caucasus University

In this book by the young financier Tamar Gakharia, which I believe will soon rise to bestseller status, unfolds the captivating and arduous journey of another strong and successful Georgian woman.

Tamar Gakharia, with an open heart and unfiltered honesty, shares personal stories from her life, unveiling the secrets behind her success and providing practical advice. The path to self-realization often demands sacrifices, which can include unsuccessful attempts and regrettable mistakes. Yet, the author held herself to exceptionally high standards, which will undoubtedly be an inspiration for other Georgian women.

"*The Blitz* is not just my story; it's a testament to the resilience of Georgian women and the nation itself. As I face the future with cautious optimism, I continue to work towards building a stronger, more prosperous Georgia, brick by brick," writes Tamar. Despite countless challenges, she persevered, forging her own destiny and crafting a tale of transformation. I am certain her journey will ignite the spirit of perseverance in many women, encouraging them to push forward and strive for their goals, no matter the obstacles they encounter.

—Natia Turnava

First Vice-Governor | Acting Governor of the National Bank of Georgia; former minister of Economy and Sustainable Development of Georgia

The Blitz is a powerful and deeply personal memoir that captures both the turbulence of post-Soviet Georgia and the unwavering resilience of an extraordinary individual. Through her courage, determination, and commitment to her family, career, and country, Tamar offers an inspiring testament to the strength of the human spirit.

—George Tkhelidze
Deputy CEO, Corporate and Investment Banking, Wealth Management; Vice President and Treasurer of American Chamber of Commerce in Georgia

THE BLITZ

TAMAR
GAKHARIA

THE
BLITZ

A GEORGIAN DAUGHTER'S
RISE AS A CFO IN THE
POST-SOVIET ERA

Forbes | Books

Published by Forbes Books, Charleston, South Carolina.
An imprint of Advantage Media Group.

Forbes Books is a registered trademark, and the Forbes Books colophon is a trademark of Forbes Media, LLC.

Printed in the United States of America.

10 9 8 7 6 5 4 3 2 1

ISBN: 979-8-88750-596-1 (Hardcover)
ISBN: 979-8-88750-597-8 (eBook)

Library of Congress Control Number: 2024922358

Cover design by Matthew Morse.
Layout design by Ruthie Wood.

Disclaimer: This book's subject matter touches upon sensitive material, including a family member's suicide. If you or someone you know is in crisis and needs help, you can contact your local emergency services or call or text 988 to connect with the 988 Suicide & Crisis Lifeline.

This custom publication is intended to provide accurate information and the opinions of the author in regard to the subject matter covered. It is sold with the understanding that the publisher, Forbes Books, is not engaged in rendering legal, financial, or professional services of any kind. If legal advice or other expert assistance is required, the reader is advised to seek the services of a competent professional.

Since 1917, Forbes has remained steadfast in its mission to serve as the defining voice of entrepreneurial capitalism. Forbes Books, launched in 2016 through a partnership with Advantage Media, furthers that aim by helping business and thought leaders bring their stories, passion, and knowledge to the forefront in custom books. Opinions expressed by Forbes Books authors are their own. To be considered for publication, please visit **books.Forbes.com**.

Contents

Introduction. 1

Chapter 1 7
Inception

Chapter 2 23
Metamorphosis

Chapter 3 31
Eyes on the Prize

Chapter 4 45
The Best-Laid Plans

Chapter 5 57
Here Comes the Bride

Chapter 6 65
The Prisoner's Wife

Chapter 7 . . . . **75**

Reunited

Chapter 8 . . . . **83**

New Dreams

Chapter 9 . . . . **91**

The Breaking Point

Chapter 10 . . . .**107**

This Is War

Chapter 11 . . . .**115**

Free at Last

Chapter 12 . . . . **125**

Facing the Future

Acknowledgments **139**

About the Author **143**

To my amazing daughter, and to all daughters and women everywhere!

From the moment you, my daughter, entered my life, you've been a constant source of inspiration, reminding me daily of the beauty, strength, and resilience that resides within the human spirit.

Your energy has propelled me to pursue my dreams and face challenges head-on.

This book chronicles my journey—a story that's as much about personal growth as it is about the values that make our nation extraordinary. As you dive into these pages, remember that our history is woven with tenacity, freedom, and boundless opportunity.

As you turn these pages, know that every decision I've made and every path I've walked was influenced by a desire to contribute to a greater cause—to brick by heavy brick build a legacy for you, rooted in the values of liberty, equality, and justice.

You are the future, with limitless potential to shape the world around you. Your boldness, compassion, and drive are exactly what this country—and the world—needs to continue thriving. I hope my experiences offer wisdom and inspiration, and perhaps at times, a gentle warning, as you carve out your own path in life. Remember, if you cannot see a better future, build one!

You, all daughters and women everywhere, who shatter glass ceilings, and who inspire those around them: you embody the strength and resilience that propel us forward. Celebrate your freedoms, uphold the values that unite us, and embrace every challenge as an opportunity to shine.

Be proud of where you come from, but never forget that your greatest duty is to where you are going. Embrace every challenge as an opportunity to build character, and approach every endeavor with an unyielding belief in your capabilities.

Your curiosity, empathy and courage are the very qualities that make life so incredibly beautiful. Walk your path with confidence, integrity, and a fearless heart. Your journey is a chapter in a much larger narrative—one that began long before us and will continue long after, full of promise and endless possibilities. Dream big, work smart, and always lead with kindness and strength.

With all my love and unwavering support,

Mom

Introduction

> ## ONE CANNOT BUILD THE QUEEN'S PALACE FROM THE RUINS OF A HEN HOUSE.
>
> ### —AKA MORCHILADZE, GEORGIAN AUTHOR AND HISTORIAN

Imagine you have a goal to build a home fit for a queen. The job would require tremendous effort, beginning with the bricks you would use to construct the walls of this home. You could not build it from bricks of sticks and clay—a palace demands better material, to form walls strong enough to stand for centuries. For that, you would need to dig deep, for the finest stone. Once you excavate it, you would need to refine it, and polish it, and carve it into bricks of the perfect size and shape. Only then, brick by heavy brick, can you begin to build that palace.

This is what it takes to build a country. And also the way I am trying to build a better life for my children, and maybe myself.

My first child, my daughter, was born on May 26, the Republic of Georgia's Independence Day. I will never forget waking up in my hospital bed in my hometown of Tbilisi, my country's capital city, opening my eyes to see three jets streaming across the sky to the west.

They were flying the colors of the Georgian flag behind them: red for the blood of our ancestors and our two thousand years of struggle, white representing peace and hope for the Georgian people. I was overcome with emotion, with love for my country and for my baby daughter.

I remembered having then written an emotional letter to the first lady of Georgia. Unexpectedly, in return, I had received a present from her in the hospital: her book, a jar with the name of my daughter on it, diapers, and other necessary things for a newborn. I burst into tears.

After reading her book, I wrote another letter of gratitude to her, also describing my thoughts about the book. At that time, I could only have dreamed of doing anything so inspirational. Now, as I am writing my own book, my only wish is to inspire at least one person in the world, to help one person grow stronger and believe in herself. Likewise, when I looked into my daughter's eyes on that day, I felt I wanted to give her everything, to be everything she needed me to be. I wanted to build her that palace.

But how could I do that? I was only twenty-three years old, living in a country that was, in a way, even younger than I was.

Despite those thousands of years of history, the Republic of Georgia of today was born out of the collapse of the Soviet Union in 1991. It hit our society like the infamous Blitz that caused chaos and destruction during the Second World War—only more powerful. Literally everything that held us together was wiped away, except for the people. We have been coming out of this blitz together, my country and me, for my entire life, experiencing years of almost constant crises and upheaval, while also finding strengths we did not know we possessed, in parallel.

When my daughter was born, nineteen years after independence, we were still searching for that stone that would provide a strong foundation. Georgia had just come through yet another period of war and was still suffering from violence, corruption, and general instability. My own life was in chaos, with my husband in jail for the second time. It was hard to find any hope or happiness. I wanted more for my baby girl. Gazing into her eyes that first time, I prayed to God to help me raise her as a free and happy person, who would be able to realize her aspirations without any influence from others.

That was my prayer for my child, and maybe, while I didn't know it, a little bit for myself. That is when I first began to think about the bricks I would need to build the palace that represented a better future for my daughter.

Today, brick by brick, I am still building that palace—and, in my own small way, helping to rebuild my country.

***

I am writing this book in English, which means there is a good chance that you, my reader, may have never heard of my country. When I tell people where I am from, they usually think I mean the US state of Georgia. I am from a country called Georgia, known to us as Sakartvelo. Some attribute this name Georgia to the Persian designation gurğ (wolf, or land of the wolves), while others believe it was named in honor of Saint George. Either way, located at the crossroads of Europe and Asia, Georgia has a history and culture dating back to ancient times, before the development of Western civilization.

Because the country is located on the trade route known as the Silk Road, which connected China to Europe and the Mediterranean Sea, people from many different civilizations passed through and settled on our land, which gives our country its unique, multicultural character. The country itself is tiny, slightly smaller than the US state of South Carolina, with a population of only 3.7 million people. It is also a breathtakingly beautiful place, filled with forested mountains, crystal rivers, ancient cities, seaside resorts, and a culture going back thousands of years. But more than that, it is my home.

It is my heart.

You might wonder why I, a tiny person, with a tiny voice, living in a tiny country many people have never even heard of, am writing a book in English. What could my story possibly mean to people outside my country, or even my region? I agree that writing a book is an unexpected undertaking for me, and I certainly do not think of myself as a hero. But I still believe my story means something. Because, in a way, it is also Georgia's story, and the history of my people and my country and our survival despite the odds is an important one to tell. Especially now, I think, when so many parts of the world are unstable, and so many people are trying to make change. There are many of us out here, not only in Georgia but also in other post-Soviet republics and other emerging nations around the world, trying to build our own palaces, trying to create a better world for our children.

So when I was approached to tell my story, to write about the small part I am playing in this undertaking, I said yes to the opportunity. Maybe I am not a hero, but if the story of how I have survived and found success and happiness under sometimes impossible circumstances (and in what is still very much a man's world) can help or inspire even one other person, how can I not tell it? That's why we live; that's why we are human beings—to share our experiences and learn from each other. So in this book, I will share a little bit of me, an ordinary Georgian girl, working to help her tiny country take its place in the bigger world.

***

My name is Tamar Gakharia, and I am currently the CFO of CBS Group, a holding company with assets in a range of sectors, including energy, communications, transportation, real estate, and more that is helping to build a modern, thriving Georgia, along with other countries in the Caucasus. I have been with the company for eleven years, ever since it was just an idea and I was just twenty-five. At the time, I had a toddler to take care of and one of the only truly stable jobs available in my country—working as the principal corporate banker for JSC Bank of Georgia. But I had a sense that this idea for a different kind of holding company that would help develop the modern systems our struggling country needed could be transformational. It could be part of building Georgia into a palace, and I wanted to be a part of it. Today, what was once just an idea is one of the top ten holding companies in Georgia, with half a billion dollars in assets. And, just like Georgia, and just like me, we are growing stronger every year.

If you had told me this fourteen years ago, when I was lying in a hospital bed with my daughter, you might as well have told me I would someday be the queen of England. I named my baby Alexsandra, or Sandra, after a saint known for legendary strength, who was tortured for her Christianity during the time of Saint George but stood strong in her faith. I chose this name for a reason. I knew that if my daughter was to live the kind of life I wanted for her growing up in a place like Georgia, she would need to be a strong woman.

My family had raised me to be a strong woman, or a strong person, since my father and grandfather believed a woman could do anything a man can do. My parents and grandparents sacrificed everything so that I could have the best education and every opportunity. For whatever reason, they believed in me—I remember my grandfather, Konstantine, telling me, when I was still very young, that I would "make change" in some way.

But life in a developing country is more about surviving than it is about making change. At the time Sandra was born, you did not know whether you would still have your job the next day. Inflation made even basic necessities like diapers unaffordable. Russian soldiers stood just twenty-three kilometers from the city, ready to come in and smash Tbilisi to bits in a single day, if they wanted to. It was hard to live your life as if it were normal. Still, in Georgia, this was normal. It was the only life any Georgian my age had ever known. So we did what we always do. We continued putting one foot in front of the other, working and dreaming and pushing us forward, into the modern world. And fourteen years later, things have gotten better. Not only is my daughter strong and thriving, but Georgia is also thriving and safer, although as I write this, we are experiencing another period of unrest. But we have come a long way in our thirty-five years as a democratic republic. Together, we are continuing to add more bricks to the wall of our palace, making it stronger and better for everyone.

This is the story of how we got here and where I hope we will go next.

Chapter 1

INCEPTION

I was four or five years old the day I saw the fire wheels. My father was driving me home from kindergarten. I was sitting next to him in the front seat of our car—there were no regulations about where a small child should sit in a car in the '90s in Georgia, so of course, I took advantage of the opportunity to sit with my dad, whom I adored, and tell him everything about my day. It was winter, so it was already dark outside as we made our way home. Then suddenly, the sky outside lit up with this strange, beautiful light. Wheels of fire were rolling toward us, down the hill between us and our apartment building.

To my kindergartner's eyes, this was an amazing sight. Who expected something so different on our boring drive home? But my father did not share my delight. Within seconds, he stopped the car, grabbed me, pulled me out, and put his coat over my head so I couldn't see what was happening. Then he took off running, carrying me, leaving his keys in the car. Suddenly, I was scared. I tried to push his coat away from my face. I cried, "Leave me alone! What is happening?" But my father just kept running, with me in his arms, saying, "Don't be afraid. Just trust me. Everything is going to be OK."

I did trust my father. I thought he was a superhero. So I stopped crying, and I was not afraid.

I remember I could see my father's feet, which were covered with dust and mud. He was carrying me with a lot of care, but I was still hit by trees, and I could tell that we were passing through some obstacles. Finally, when we were in the middle of a park with a lot of trees, he pulled the coat from my head so I could see. Then we ran home together, maybe three or four kilometers, to our apartment building on the other side of the hill.

That night, in my room, I heard my father, in my parents' room next door, talking to my mother, explaining what had happened. He told her we were stopped by people who wanted to steal our car, just like someone who had been killed on the street for their car the month before. I remember my mother went to an altar we had in our apartment and prayed to God, thanking him for sparing us.

The next day, my father found his car, maybe half a kilometer away from the place where we left it. It was totally without wheels, without a radio, without seats, without everything. It was only the metal shell of the car, burned from the firebombs.

There was nothing left for the thieves to drive away.

***

If you live in the West, you probably remember the fall of the Soviet Union as a great moment—a historical triumph that was cheered across the globe. But supporting a revolution and celebrating its success is one thing. Living through the collapse of your society and the loss of everything a government does for its people is something else entirely. In Georgia, we understand the price of freedom because our parents' generation paid for it with everything they had.

In the midtwentieth century, Georgia was one of the most prosperous countries in the USSR. Our location at the crossroads of Europe and Asia, our mild climate due to our location between the Black Sea and the Caucasus Mountains, our abundant agriculture (including an eight-thousand-year history of wine making), and our modern industry built through Soviet investment all contributed to what was a relatively stable way of life. Parents knew that their children would be educated and that their families would not starve. No one had to worry about having a place to live. Crime was, for the most part, controlled, although the methods could be harsh, and government corruption was always a problem.

But in a way, all of this was meaningless, because the people were not free. They were fed and housed, and they were educated, but they were not allowed to make their own choices or pursue their own dreams. Under the Soviet system, the government made those decisions for you.

My family had what constituted a "good life," in part because, like many Georgians, they were highly educated. My parents, Robert and Mary, are both doctors. My father's father, my grandfather Konstantine, was the prosecutor in our area of Tbilisi, and my grandmother had been an accountant. My mother's parents were both engineers. They were what passed for higher society in a Communist system—they had good jobs, they had good incomes, and they were able to invest in property that they owned, save money, and plan for the future.

But they also knew that their future was limited to what was allowed under the system. And that system strived for sameness. Soviet life was a celebration of conformity, with silence—damned, godless silence—the Soviets' favorite form of music. People from my parents' generation say it was like living in a world where everything was gray. No other colors existed, there was no rainbow … and any deviation, exception, or differentiation was punished. So people accepted this gray, monotonous-yet-stable existence, just to stay safe and live their lives and avoid trouble. As George Orwell once wrote, "The choice for mankind lies between freedom and happiness and for the great bulk of mankind, happiness is better." Unfortunately.

Then, in the 1980s, cracks began to form in the system. There was economic stagnation and growing unrest across the Soviet Union as the Cold War, among other factors, took its toll. Prices skyrocketed, living standards plummeted, and the stability people had known for decades started to slip away. More people started questioning their leaders. Why should they be forced to live these gray, dismal lives, following rules that stifled their dreams, when they couldn't afford enough to eat? More people began to stand up and demand their freedom, and a wave of nationalism rose across the Soviet republics—especially in Georgia, among the educated and the younger generation.

I was born in 1987, just before the blitz that wiped the Soviet Union away.

The independence movement picked up steam in 1988, as young people and members of the intelligentsia embraced this "national awakening." There were demonstrations for independence and crack-downs, followed by bigger demonstrations and bigger crackdowns. Then, on April 9, 1989, a red line was crossed. In the center of Tbilisi—again, the capital city where my family lived—Soviet soldiers were sent to disperse a large crowd of peaceful protesters. The scene turned violent. Twenty-one people died, most of them young, sixteen of them women. Hundreds more were injured. The brutality was shocking. These were innocent people, bludgeoned and bloodied and shot, just for speaking out. The violence united all of Georgia against the Soviets. It was not only "first blood" in our country; April 9, 1989, was the beginning of the end of the USSR.

***

Even as a toddler, I was aware that our situation was difficult. So when my mother got pregnant with my little brother, I was upset. I assessed the situation in a rational way, figuring that another person in the family would take things away from me, like my sweets and my toys. When my baby brother was announced, I was already not a fan … and then he almost took my mother from me. After a difficult labor and delivery in a hospital that had no water or power, she contracted an infection and almost died. I'll never forget her face when my father and I went to the hospital to visit her. We were not allowed to go in, only to look in through a window. She was covered with sweat.

It took me years to forgive poor Konstantine for that.

***

The year of my brother's birth turned out to be an eventful one. On November 14, 1990, we named our new country the Republic of Georgia. On April 9, 1991, after a national referendum, Georgia officially declared independence from the Soviet Union, becoming the first non-Baltic state to do so. Eight months later, on Christmas Day, Gorbachev resigned as leader of the Soviet Union, and on December 31, 1991, the Union of Soviet Socialist Republics ceased to exist.

The newly rechristened Republic of Georgia was finally free, but we were also in turmoil. Our currency lost 76 percent of its value in a single day and was eventually abandoned, so people were given tickets, or coupons, to trade for bread and milk. The price of bread rose a hundred times higher, while the average salary fell to around three dollars. Civil war broke out, and much of the country, including the streets of Tbilisi, became a war zone, with neighborhood gangs killing each other and robbing and sometimes killing ordinary citizens, sometimes for something as basic as a loaf of bread.

I remember being terrified at night, even before the fire wheels, from the sounds of explosions and shooting. We lived on the first floor, which made us vulnerable to these gangsters, who would take everything from our home, sometimes when we were sleeping, sometimes when we were away visiting family. At one point, my father decided it would be pointless to replace the front window again, because the gangsters were always breaking it. He covered it with plywood that I remember writing on with chalk, trying to record the schedule of when we did and did not have electricity. There was no rational explanation for when the power would come and when it could go away, but I tried to find one anyway.

Many people left the country for the West during this period of instability. My uncle, who is also a doctor, moved to Sweden in the '80s, even before Georgia became independent, and still lives there today. But my parents chose to remain in their homeland. They understood that we were in a turbulent situation, but they also understood the importance of this transition period and that we needed to be strong. They were eager to be a part of rising from the blitz to create a new Georgia, to raise their children in a free country, and to help ensure our national identity survived. They were, like all the Georgians who stayed, our heroes. They are why we became free.

My parents stayed in our home in Tbilisi, even though it was not always safe there, so my mother could continue to go to the hospital and do her job, even if she had to wait months to get paid for her work. And my father continued to go to work and do his job until, after a while, he did not have a job to go to, and then he found other ways to contribute.

They knew that if they gave up, then the whole country would give up.

My father was a psychiatrist, the head of his department. As you might imagine, mental health was not a tremendous priority in a country where people could not afford bread (even though, perhaps, it should have been), so little by little, year by year, the facility where he worked closed down until my father had no work left to do or workplace to go to. He became an entrepreneur, looking for new ways to supplement my mother's less-than-regular income and make life easier for our fellow Georgians.

For example, after the collapse of the Soviet Union, there was no infrastructure, no supply chain, to bring in the medicine people needed, even for a headache. So my father traveled to India to import it. He began exporting nuts and tried to cultivate sugar because there was a big black market for food; whatever you did not grow yourself, you had to wait in line for—one endless line for bread, another endless line for milk. People would sometimes wait all day long until they stopped handing out bread and milk at six o'clock at night. If your parents came home without it, it meant that they did not manage to get in line early enough. And even if they managed to get bread and milk, someone might come up to them with a gun and take it away.

But there were many more people who did not want to rob and kill, who wanted to build a strong and free Georgia. And those people banded together. When my father did well in his export-and-import business and managed to buy supplies outside of Georgia, or when he was somehow able to get a lot of food tickets, he would put all the food in his car and share it with all the neighbors on our block. There was a communal spirit among the people. The times were difficult, but we were working to get through them together, to somehow survive and hopefully create a better country for the next generation.

***

When I was very little, my father's parents lived in our apartment with us, and my grandmother Tina looked after me while my parents worked. However, my grandfather Konstantine was building a house in a village called Mukhuri, 278 kilometers to the west of Tbilisi at the foot of the Caucasus Mountains, where he and my grandmother were born and raised. He started building it before the Soviet Union collapsed, because he saw what was coming and wanted to be ready. When he lost his job as a prosecutor, which he eventually did when the Soviet Union collapsed, his plan was to work as a lawyer in the countryside, because there was a big knowledge gap between the capital city and the villages. In fact, many people were leaving the city for the countryside. With our infrastructure gone, we had begun to rely on the country to feed the capital, so those who had land to cultivate went to grow food.

Even before the house was finished, we would travel to Mukhuri every summer. We lived with a neighboring family in the summers before our house was built, and my grandparents had helped this family a lot. They gave them housing in Tbilisi and supported them financially to get higher education in the capital. Though this couple never had children of their own, they treated my brother and me as their own.

The husband was a veterinarian. From him, I learned a love for animals—how to treat them, how to milk a cow or look after a beehive. Later, when my grandfather decided to have beehives, I already was a professional beekeeper and helped him, even extracting honey independently.

His wife taught me to cook delicious Mingrelian food and how to do housework and garden, and she helped me with summer assignments and read so many books to me when I was a small girl. Thinking on it now, I remember that she was an accountant and took me to work with her; I loved looking over her calculations, seeing how everything balances when it's all correct. These basic principles of accounting have, of course, influenced my profession, but every other aspect of my life as well: everything must have balance, and if you want to keep it, you should keep moving!

The trip to Mukhuri was long and dangerous, but it meant we'd get to spend time in the safety of the country—it sometimes took ten hours, because so many roads were destroyed and there was no infrastructure, and you could be stopped at any time for any reason. But it was worth it, especially after my grandparents' house was finished in 1991. My grandfather built it next to a stream, and it was the first in the village to have a bathroom inside the house.

My grandfather began working as a lawyer, and my grandmother grew fresh fruits and vegetables and corn to send to us, along with cheese and honey. I remember how excited I would get when the parcels would arrive filled with my favorite homemade sweets—one made with grape syrup and nuts, another a fruit porridge that was dried and rolled. Sometimes I would get a letter that was addressed only to me from my grandmother, which was very special.

Everyone in the area around the village knew my grandparents. My grandmother was known for being generous—they did not have a lot, but they had more than most people, so she was always giving people money or food. When people asked my grandfather for food, he would try to get them to work, giving them seeds and telling them to plant them and grow something for themselves. Then they would turn around and ask my grandmother, and she would feel sorry for them, go to the mill to get flour, and bring it home and make bread for them.

I spent every summer in the countryside with my father's parents, and while I missed my mother and father, those months spent hiking and riding horses and climbing trees were magical. My grandfather Konstantine believed, and told me frequently, that women and men were equal, and he instilled in me from an early age that I could do whatever I wanted to do with my life and be whatever I wanted to be. He even told me it wouldn't matter if I got married a hundred times if that was what it took for me to be happy, which was a pretty revolutionary point of view for a Georgian man his age. Even in the twenty-first century, girls were expected to find husbands and have babies and not much more.

So ever since those early days, I have enjoyed writing and numbers. Whenever I look at financial statements, numbers tell me a story. Age, for instance, was never a mere number for me, as I always presented it as a unit of experience. It is the same in business. You create something that is ultimately a number, representing the return on the work you put in.

I was at my grandparents' house when I first grasped the principal of supply and demand. I wanted to eat khachapuri, a delicious Georgian cheese-filled bread, but my grandma had nothing but flour. At the same time, some of my neighbors had cheese, and others had eggs. To solve this imbalance, I would go on a journey with my grandfather to Lugela Canyon to fish for some trout. I used the fish as a commodity to barter with our neighbors for eggs and cheese. With all the ingredients, my grandma made the khachapuri, which we all enjoyed (and which, it turns out, is a lot like sharing shareholder value and capitalizing on investment!). Climbing those beautiful gorges as a little girl and standing in crystal clear, icy water with a mission in mind and a long spinner bait in my hands, I had a feeling of accomplishment that has given me strength, even in my darkest moments.

By the way, khachapuri is so ubiquitous in Georgia that the price of making it is used as a measure of inflation called the "Khachapuri Index." So I am not the only Georgian to see a link between our national cheese bread and the economy!

My grandfather did not see me as some delicate little flower. He would take me out hunting and fishing in the mountains, just like he took my brother. He taught me to shoot a gun and to catch fish with my hands, like a bear. Later, he made me my own little fishing pole. I adored eating the fish I caught—I felt like I was a hero and the best fisher ever. He taught me how to drive a car when I was only ten years old, plus how to change a tire and, later, to rebuild a car engine and to carve a chair out of wood. It was an incredible education in life and was all for a specific reason; after everything my grandfather had seen and survived, he wanted his granddaughter to be ready for anything. He always said, "No one knows what the future will look like, so you should know everything." Looking back, I think that his real goal was to teach me to know who I am and to have self-confidence. I would not be the woman I am today without his influence.

***

My other grandparents, my mother's parents, lived in the central city, in a much more desirable neighborhood than the suburb where my parents lived. When I entered first grade, I was sent to live with them, because one of the best public schools in Tbilisi was in their neighborhood, and my mother wanted me to go to that school. That's how focused my parents were on my education, even in a country full of turmoil. Thinking back on it, I realize it was kind of crazy. In addition to school, I had English language classes, tennis lessons, swimming classes, karate classes, dance classes, and arts and crafts classes. I did winter sports, I rode horses ... I had a million different activities, just like any over-scheduled Western child. But I did not have smooth paper to write my homework on or heat to keep my fingers from cramping in the cold.

I knew my mother wanted the best for me, and I wanted to be good for my mother. I saw how hard she worked and how hard both of my parents struggled, and I felt it deeply. However, I was only a young girl, and I didn't want to leave the home where I was born and raised, even though my mother thought it was best for me. I didn't want to leave my neighborhood friends. I didn't want my little brother to have my parents all to himself. And I really didn't want to live with my grandmother because she was very strict.

My mother's mother was Russian, highly educated and cultured, with expectations to match. She was beautiful—I remember men coming to our home and saying, "Please leave your husband and marry me. I have millions of coupons I am ready to give to you." That was what passed for romance in Georgia in the 1990s. Not flowers or candy. Coupons. Her husband, my grandfather, came from what was considered a noble family and had held executive positions in many different factories and organizations during Soviet times. He was the life of the party and very generous—the kind of person who would give their last penny to a stranger. My grandmother was always yelling at him about that.

The best thing about my mother's mother was that she never lied. Whether it was good or bad, she always told the truth, not only to me, but also to everyone. I think that part of her is in me. I always tell the truth, whether it is in a diplomatic way or not. She taught me the feminine side of how to be a strong woman, providing me with a classical education, giving me books to read and exposing me to culture in the form of music, dance, and art. But I did not always appreciate her efforts. I missed my parents, even though I saw them every weekend. And I did not like my new school because my fellow students were all snobs.

The children in my grandparents' neighborhood were different from the kids in my part of Tbilisi. If your father didn't have a car or you were not dressed in good clothes, you did not fit in. I was also bullied because I came from the countryside—they would call me a country girl and say my father was a peasant—specifically a Mingrelian, from a part of western Georgia with its own language where myths like Jason and the Golden Fleece and the story of Medea were born. It's certainly not a bad culture to come from—it's the ancient land of Colchis, and Colchian women were always considered the most beautiful and intelligent in the region. But because of tensions dating back to Georgia's first civil war when we lost Abkhazia—when some criminal groups led by Mingrelians terrorized civilians—and because Mingrelians have their own language, they were always considered separate and different from "regular Georgians."

This did not matter to me; I was proud of my ancestors, my grandparents, and my village where I spent every summer. But it was difficult for me to be myself and show my personality to people who were constantly picking on me. I was bullied for everything—because my grandmother was Russian and because I did not look Georgian, with my Slavic features like white skin, light-colored eyes, and a more pointed nose. So I hated going to school. And sometimes, I would put the thermometer on the radiator or rub it between my palms to make it hot, and my grandmother would see I had a fever and tell my mother I was sick, and she would leave work and come rushing over to take care of me. It worked every time … for a while.

School under what remained of the Soviet system was very rigorous. We were given homework to do over the weekend—the very first week of school! I remember going back home after that first, endless, horrible week of class, with all those terrible, mean children, and all I wanted to do was play. I sat in the middle of the floor and spread my entire bounty of cars and toys and dolls all around me. My mother walked in, took one look at the scene, and asked, "Don't you have homework to do?"

I decided to protest. "Sorry, Mom, but school is not for me. Look at me. I'm a small girl, and what makes me happy is just to sit and play and not to study." I was, in fact, a very cute, small girl, with shining dark hair and green eyes. I smiled my most winning smile and said, "Please, Mom, make me happy."

My mother replied that if I didn't study, I would not get good grades.

I thought about that for a moment. If I was not a good girl like my mother wanted me to be, would I have to live at my grandmother's all my life? For the first time, I considered that maybe it was more important for me to make my mother happy than it was for her to make me happy. From that day on, I took school seriously. I studied every weekend. And I actually loved all the subjects, especially doing math, studying nature, and writing stories and poems. I did very well and always had the highest grades.

By the time I finished first grade, I had a best friend, who lived in the apartment next door to my grandmother's. We were in the same class and did everything together, and my grandparents knew her family, so she was almost like family to me. We used to go into my grandmother's room and steal her clothes, these beautiful scarves and necklaces and earrings, and dress up and pretend to be princesses. We would go out in the streets dressed in all these grown-up clothes and jewelry, dancing and performing and asking people for candy. We thought we were great. Once I lost one of my grandmother's precious earrings, and after I got caught, I had to stand in a corner for three hours, begging for release.

My grandmother was a talented seamstress, and she would sew beautiful white skirts and dresses, with incredible detail and ornamentation, for me to wear to school. She would get very upset if I came home with dirt on my beautiful dress. But I was quite an active child, which made avoiding dirt basically impossible. So I came up with a solution. I found some training clothes someone had thrown in the trash and hid them in a special place on my way to school. Every day, I would change out of the beautiful clothes that my grandmother made and hide them in this secret spot and put on my garbage clothes to go to school. The clothes were too big for me, maybe twice as big as I was, but I didn't care. Until my teacher called my mother and said, "That poor girl, coming to school in the same clothes every day that aren't even hers!" She thought I was so poor, she was ready to adopt me. She even bought me some clothes. All because I thought my grandmother would kill me if I got my dress dirty.

***

Outdoor fun could only be had during the daytime, because that was the only time it was safe to be outside. Children were regularly kidnapped for ransom, and some were even killed. This was so common that the brother of one of our current mayors was kidnapped and killed during this period. Going out after dark was not a good idea for anyone, especially a child. However, in the daytime, with our parents away at work, with no cell phones, it was a different world. If you were able to get the OK from an adult to go out, you had total freedom to do anything you wanted.

We would play in the yards of our apartment buildings, where there was space to play with a ball or with elastics, which were these long rubber bands we used for a jump-rope-type game. Garbage was everywhere, including things like engines and radiators, and we would dismantle them and pull out the tin, which we could bend and mold into toy soldiers and cars. I had a lot of toys I found on the street, including a collection of shell casings from bullets from all the shootings in the area. I organized them all by the name of the gun, the factory where they were made, and the year.

We did so many things that my parents even now don't know. For example, I was maybe eight or nine when I first found out how babies were made. In residential buildings in Tbilisi, the first floor was typically built as the "commercial floor"—with spaces filled with markets and stores. After the Soviet Union fell, those businesses were all abandoned, and less-reputable, black-market enterprises moved in … including, in a building not far from my grandparents' home, a "house" of prostitution. My friends and I would watch the sex workers and their customers through a peephole, just like Robert DeNiro in the movie *Once Upon a Time in America*. I knew each and every neighbor who was cheating on his wife.

Some people in the neighborhood had private houses with vegetable gardens, and we would climb in and hide without permission, taking the vegetables and fruits and eating them without washing them, like rabbits. We had no money for treats like chewing gum, so we would pick up black tar off the street and chew that. It was actually very pleasant to chew. I think it was popular among post-Soviet children. I loved sweets of any kind, and my absolute favorite sweet was a biscuit or cookie that, if you put it next to a flame, would catch on fire like a piece of paper. To this day, I have no idea what that sweet was made of or what I was eating, although it had to be better than chewing tar.

Sometimes I don't know how I survived. But I did.

Chapter 2

METAMORPHOSIS

I often say my parents' generation paid the cost of Georgia's freedom. I also knew this cost. I felt it when I spent nights doing my homework by the light of an oil lamp that filled the room with toxic fumes and made my eyes water because we had no electricity for light or heat, but the homework still had to be done. I felt it when my parents left home early in the morning and worked long into the night, but sometimes there was still not enough food to eat. I felt that life was hard, and some kind of price was being paid. What I could not understand was what we were paying for. I did not yet understand the concept of freedom.

Our parents did. They knew that while the price was steep, freedom meant everything.

***

One day, when I was in the third grade, my mother sat me down for a serious talk. She told me that she and my father were both concerned about my not living with them and that there was a very nice school about to open near our neighborhood. This school might be more challenging for me than the public school because it was an Italian school. I might struggle to keep up with my lessons, and I might miss my friends. But I would have an opportunity to make new friends and get a good education, and maybe even go to Italy to study in a few years if I did well.

Also, I would be able to live with my parents again.

That was all that mattered to me. From that moment on, I was constantly asking my mother when I would be starting my new school.

The school, one of the first and best private schools in Georgia, was (and is) run by the Georgian Italian Society. It was created to give the refugees from the wars that happened after the fall of the Soviet Union a good Western education. For those refugee students, the school was free of charge, but it also accepted paying, nonrefugee students like me. Of course, my parents had no money for tuition at a private school. But my mother knew that this school would give me opportunities no other school could. She saw it as the key to unlocking the kind of future she wanted for me, the kind she never could have herself. So she gave an ultimatum to my father that I was going to attend that school, no matter what. And I was able to move back home.

My family began what would ultimately be a yearslong process of divesting their fortune to invest in my future. I use that term "fortune" loosely. Accumulating vast amounts of wealth was not possible under the Soviet system, and most of whatever wealth people had accumulated was used up in the years after the collapse to pay for basic necessities. But everyone in my family still found something to contribute to my education. My mother's mother sold her first of many packets of shares in the engineering conglomerate she had worked for. My father's mother sold her antiques. My mother sold the jewelry my father had given her during Soviet times and even had her gold teeth removed. Because of their sacrifices, I was able to go to the Italian school.

That's when my real transformation started.

***

When I moved back home, I was so glad to be there that I was even happy to see my little brother. But I was not nearly as happy as Konstantine was. From the moment I got back, he always wanted to be by my side, to share the same chair where I was sitting and studying, to share my blanket while he had his own bed. Life was a constant fight for space, for toys, for attention, for treats, for everything. Sometimes, the battles were not so serious, like when I shot Konstantine with the little plastic balls from his toy gun. Other times, it was more serious—like the time I broke his finger or another time when I broke his nose. He must have loved me very much, because instead of telling my parents, he protected me and lied about falling or walking into a wall or something. He was my partner in crime, and I was killing him! I really loved him, too, even though he annoyed me.

I also loved my new school. There were only ten students in my fourth-grade class, where in my public school, there had been forty. But I was also the only student in the class who did not speak Italian. In the beginning, my classmates were all refugees, and they had already spent some time living in Italy with Italian host families. That meant they knew, at a minimum, enough Italian to communicate. I knew exactly three words: pizza, spaghetti, and ciao. If I had any hope of succeeding at this school, I had to learn the language—especially since some of the books and classes were in Italian. So I went through my house and put stickers on everything with the Italian word for that thing; for example, the table had a sticker with the word tavola on it. This drove my mother crazy, but I was determined to do well and be the top student in the school, or at least succeed enough where I would not wind up back in the public school, living with my grandmother. Luckily, my training method worked. I was able to master the language and find my way back to the spot where I felt most comfortable—at the top of my class.

***

A few months after I started at the Italian school, a dance teacher came through, looking for students to join a dance class. She looked over different children, and when she got to me, she told me I was a good dancer—good enough that she later spoke to my mother and told her that I should dance professionally. I began taking classes in Georgian folk dance with this teacher after school ... classes my mother also had to pay for. My family sold more of their valuables, and another door opened for me.

I was only nine or ten years old when my dance group went on a bus trip, performing across Greece and Bulgaria. It was my first trip without my parents, and it was so exciting—we went with our whole dance squad, our teachers, and the live musicians who accompanied us when we danced. I was the youngest member of our group.

The trip to Bulgaria took about four days, and we spent most of the time on that bus. It had two levels, with a kitchenette and a bathroom upstairs. My mother had packed five days' worth of food that was not perishable that I could cook in the microwave. We did almost everything we needed to do on the road, although sometimes we would stop at a bus station, and I would take a shower with the sink where you wash your hands.

It was such a great adventure, to travel such a huge distance on those endless roads, and then to see so many different cities in such a short period of time—a new city almost every day. It was exhausting but always exciting and interesting, learning about different lifestyles and performing for crowds of people, and meeting fellow performers from other countries like Germany and Italy.

My mother also enrolled me in drama classes, which led to my first trip to Italy, also by bus. I was recruited to be part of a company performing a play of Pinocchio at a festival. The play was in Italian, and since I was learning Italian in school, I was a perfect addition to the cast and played several roles. Once again, I was the smallest performer in our group, so my drama teacher, who wrote and directed the play, looked out for me during the trip. When I got sick on the ferry between Greece and Italy, with a fever of forty degrees Celsius, I made him promise me that if I died, he would please bring me back to Georgia to my parents. I was an actress, so I could be a little bit dramatic.

We met people from all different parts of the world at the festival—not just Europe, but as far away as Japan and China. And our group won, which was exciting. I felt noticed and good at what I did.

Looking back, I see how those experiences prepared me for the life I have today. I did not become a professional dancer or actress, but I did learn skills that have been essential to me in the real world, from reading and performing scenes that exposed me to all different cultures to getting up and speaking and performing in front of hundreds of people. I learned how to control my emotions—to cry when I did not feel like crying, and how not to cry when I wanted to. I stretched my imagination in every direction—since I was so small and flexible, I played a lot of animal roles, which gave me the chance to be creative and invent entertaining things that an animal might do. Regularly performing activities like these sharpened my ability to think outside the box. It was on-the-job training in problem-solving.

I also learned how to be part of a team, to adapt to all different surroundings, full of adult people, and to handle grown-up stresses like not sleeping every night, being away from home, and having a job people relied on me to do well. It taught me perseverance and resilience and probably a hundred other important things I'm forgetting as I write this. But one thing I can never forget is how much fun it was. What little girl from a poor country gets to dress up in beautiful costumes and travel to different countries and perform for people and have them clap and cheer for her and tell her she's great? It gave my childhood this touch of magic, despite all the hardship. It also kept me focused on the new challenges and new experiences that kept coming up for me, and on the possibilities and opportunities the future might hold.

A lot of my peers growing up with me in Georgia did not have that focus. Many had parents who were not as strong as mine were, who had given in to despair, or who were addicted to alcohol or drugs. Some of my friends had terrible parents who hit them all the time; those friends would run away to my house to hide. I did not understand that this was not normal. It did not happen to me, but it was happening all around me. So many of my friends ended up lost, involved in street crime, gambling, or addicted—not because they were bad people, but because they could see no other opportunities. They did not have a family that would sacrifice everything for them the way my family did for me.

***

I did well enough at the Italian school that I qualified for the exchange program in Italy, which began in seventh grade, when I was twelve. That was the first time I flew on a plane. Even though the Soviets were gone and our borders were free, this was still a very difficult undertaking. There was no real transportation infrastructure, so the planes were not very safe, and there were no direct flights anywhere. My parents had to come up with the money for the plane ticket, which thankfully was the only thing my family had to pay for, but then, because our monetary system was so unreliable, they had trouble proving they actually had the funds in their account. Also, because our government was so unstable, Georgia was classified as a high-risk country, so I had to get a visa in addition to my passport, and I had to get it through the consulate of France, because there was no Italian consulate in Georgia. That meant waiting in multiple queues and filling out lots of documents. But eventually, we got through it all, and I packed my things and got ready to study abroad.

I was excited but also a little bit nervous to leave. I had never been away from my family or my country for more than a month before. I had never lived with a family of strangers before. Never mind that ... I had never been on an airplane.

I remember boarding the plane with seven other students from the Italian school and one teacher. Our seats were not all together; they were scattered around the cabin, and when I found mine, I was by myself on the aisle, next to a man with white hair. This man, whom I assumed was very old but was probably not, was sitting next to the window. That was where I wanted to be. So I approached this man with white hair and told him, in a very polite voice, that it was my first time ever on an airplane, and asked if he could please change seats with me so I could see the clouds outside. He smiled and changed seats without any hesitation, and I moved next to the window to begin my adventure.

Then reality set in.

I had heard all the stories about people being afraid of flying, and now the plane was moving, and it was too late to turn back! I started praying silently to God, bargaining with him. It's a big plane,

I reasoned. There are probably some kind people on the plane you will want to save. Just in case he didn't want to save me specifically.

The plane started moving faster down the runway, which felt different from anything I had ever felt before; it was so fast, and there were so many bumps. I was so scared of what was coming next. I closed my eyes, wondering what it would feel like when we actually left the ground. I was breathing so hard that I was almost hyperventilating when I felt the plane lift into the air. I didn't know anything about flying, so I didn't swallow or open my mouth to relieve the pressure on my ears, and they really hurt.

But then the plane straightened out. It got smoother and calmer. I opened my eyes and looked out the window …

… and, oh my God, it was amazing.

I saw the trees and the houses below me and then this ocean of white clouds underneath us. I imagined myself watching my plane from the outside, visualizing it floating in this beautiful white ocean of clouds. I had grown up believing angels were sitting on the clouds, but now that I was up there, I did not see any angels. But I did see how small the world was and that all the borders that divide us into different countries and different people were artificial. In that moment, on that plane, without any attachment to the ground, I felt like a part of the whole world, not just some tiny person from a tiny country no one knew about. I felt connected to everything, and at the same time, free in a way I had never felt before, like there were endless opportunities in front of me, and all I had to do was reach out and grab them.

Chapter 3

EYES ON THE PRIZE

The first thing I noticed about Italy was that people there were all happy. Everywhere I went, I saw colorful, smiling faces; colorful, stylish clothes; colorful bicycles; and small, colorful cars. Even the food was both colorful and delicious, and the bread was from heaven. Oh my God, that bread. When my mother asked me what I remembered most about Italy, it was the smell and the taste of the bread.

Beyond the sights and smells and tastes, there was also a sense of calm I had never seen or experienced before. Italy has never been one of the calmest countries in Europe, and where I was living, the far north, was considered the "workaholic" part of the country. Still, there was an overriding absence of stress. No one seemed worried about anything. Even lower-income people seemed relaxed and unbothered. They would lie on the beautiful green grass and stare at the sun and do nothing. Nothing!

I had never imagined the possibility of a life that would allow me to do nothing.

For people my age, it was as if stress were canceled. Nobody was worried about homework or grades or what university they were going to go to—let alone how they would pay for it—like my friends in Georgia. Young people worried about where they would go that evening, or what to eat, or how to entertain, or whom to date. They had time to play. They had time to go outside, to watch TV, to go shopping ... whatever they wanted to do.

It was like seeing real freedom for the first time.

***

I lived with a host family in a town called Borgomanero, outside Milan. The mother was a math teacher from my school, and the father was an engineer for Ferrari, so they were very well off, well educated, and well mannered. They had two boys, one a year older than I was and one four years younger, and a grandmother. They were lovely and kind and everything you could want in a host family.

But I still got homesick. I was only twelve, and I had never been away from my family for so long. And calling Georgia to talk to them was so expensive. My parents had scrimped and saved to give me one hundred US dollars, a fortune to them, to spend during my time in Italy. A cell-phone card cost thirty dollars for only fifteen or twenty minutes of calls. I called them every second day and only talked for a minute or two, just to say hello and that I was OK.

My host family did everything they could to make me comfortable, but I was always aware that I was living in a different culture. Italians had different manners and attitudes than Georgians, including a lot of kissing hello, which made me uncomfortable, and rules about when it was OK to take toys and things, which I needed to get used to. I also had to get used to different foods, including some I had never tried before. I liked pasta, but I wasn't used to eating it before every meal, and with so many different kinds of sauce. I liked some better than others, but I did not want to offend my hosts, so I tried to eat everything, even if I had to force it down.

School was also a challenge. Not academically—I already knew calculus at twelve because that's typical of Soviet-style education, which amazed my teachers. But socially, Italy really was the Wild West for me. My fellow students were already smoking, already sexually active, doing things I couldn't even imagine doing at that age. I knew what sex was; my mother had explained everything when I was in fourth or fifth grade, in a very scientific way. But while I never thought sex was something bad, I was also not especially curious to try it. Unlike the Italian girls, I had many, many things I had to worry about. There was no room for boys on that list.

I was lucky, because boys did not bother me for those first few years, in Italy or at home. I still played football with the boys, I played detective games with them, and since I did not get my period until I was sixteen, I stayed skinny and flat chested, like I was one of them. I knew they thought I was pretty. They told me they liked the color of my eyes, and my skin, and the fact that I was tall, with a nose that was not big and sharp. But they were more like big brothers to me, and I was their partner in crime, even stealing my dad's playing cards with pictures of nude women on them when they started getting interested in sex. In return, when I was bullied, they would come to my rescue. They were like my squad, always ready to help me. They would do everything for me, from carrying my books home from school to confronting girls who tried to make my life hell.

I was bullied a lot by the girls in Italy, especially as we got older. Looking back, I imagine they did not understand a girl like me, who was not only from a strange country but also not interested in sex or romance, only in studying. But I did not know this at the time. All I knew was that one of these girls thought she was in love with one of my good friends, and because of this, she decided to make my life hell. She and her friends all bullied me in the corridors of the school, yelling, "The virgin is coming!" whenever I walked by.

I was fifteen the first time one of my friends told me he loved me. I saw this boy drawing my portrait on his desk, and I asked him what the hell he was doing, and he told me he had been in love with me for years. I had no idea. That was when I realized it was probably time to stop spending so much time with the boys, although by this point, I had no free time anyway, because I only had two years left before university, and after Italy, I knew I wanted to do well enough to study abroad. So I studied constantly. Even by sixteen, when boys were following me everywhere, finding out where I lived, and calling my phone number, I built a wall against them. I had a plan for my life. I could think about love stories later.

***

I went to Italy at the same time every year for five years, during the late spring, at the end of the second semester of the school year. I alternated with my first host family and the family of an Italian teacher whose husband had a business restoring antiques. They had four children—a boy in his twenties, a girl who was three years older than I, another boy who was a year or so younger than the girl, and finally a boy who was only three or four. I loved them just like I loved my first host family. When I got older, I transferred to a school in Novara, and the girl from this host family went with me. It was interesting spending time with kids who were slightly older than I was and seeing how they lived and planned for their futures.

We went on excursions all around Italy, and I got to know the country from the highest part, where I lived, to the bottom. Wherever I went, I saw a life that was so different from my life in Georgia. There was so much opportunity. It felt like you could grasp anything; you could be good at anything if you tried hard. In my country, even if you tried your hardest, you could end up with total disappointment. I decided I wanted a Western, European education, to give me the most opportunity possible. But I never considered leaving Georgia forever. I knew whatever success I had would mean nothing without my parents, without my brother, without the people I loved. Even as a teenager, I knew my homeland was not only where I paid my taxes, but where I had my heart.

I would come home from Italy in early summer, and often, our Italian host families would follow. Even though we had far less in terms of resources, we would welcome them into our homes just like they welcomed me. In Georgia, we say the guest is from God—it is in our blood. Even if we don't have a penny, we will host you as if you were a king. So we would accommodate these entire families in our very small apartment. My brother and I would vacate our room for our guests and sleep in our parents' room. Our visitors never stayed as long as I stayed in Italy, usually ten days to two weeks, because these trips did not involve any class time. Instead, we had a heavy schedule packed with gastronomic trips and excursions to the wineries and cultural and natural sights.

My Italian host families fell in love with Georgia's wild, natural beauty. We are a tiny country, but so much of it is untouched by progress, and that can have an upside. They would return year after year, sometimes traveling to different regions on their own to hike or visit cultural sites. And when there was progress made in our country, they always noticed—they would get even more excited than we did when they could come back and see a building where nothing had been the year before, or a road that had been destroyed repaired. They also loved Georgian food—we used to send them back to Italy with bags stuffed with three to five kilos of different delicacies (but probably not our bread). My mother gave them some of her antique silver jewelry—she would have given them anything, she was so grateful for the opportunity they were giving my brother, who was also part of the Italian school program, and me. All our families grew so close. Even the people who didn't speak each other's language could all understand each other without my help—just gestures and expressions were enough. Our families still have this deep connection today.

***

During the summer, in the village with my grandfather, I saw another view of life that was different from what I saw at home or in Italy. The countryside was where I saw true, raw poverty, where people struggled and worked with their hands for next to nothing. These were my grandfather's people and the people he returned to his village to help as a lawyer, working on everything ranging from defending petty criminals to helping settle land disputes. He put me to work for him every summer—since there was no electricity, every case was handwritten, and my job was to rewrite everything for him. Today I realize he probably did this not only to help him manage his time but also to teach me about his profession. While my doctor parents wanted me to follow in their footsteps, my grandfather knew me well enough to know medicine was not in my future.

My feelings toward the medical profession bordered on hatred. There may have been a point around when I was twelve or thirteen, when I thought maybe I could compromise and become a pediatrician. I love children, and that would be a way I could do the thing that my parents wanted me to do, but in my own way. But most of the time, I felt like my parents had been stolen from me by their patients and that doctors were not even really allowed to be parents, since they always had to be available to answer calls and run to see whoever called them in the middle of the night. They never had a weekend. And for all their hard work, they didn't have any money! In Georgia, medicine is one of the lowest paid professions, along with teaching—even today. You can make more money working in a supermarket than you can as a neurologist, like my mother.

At least my mother's job was secure. She had been working for the Institution of Neurology, but after the Soviet Union fell, all those national institutions started falling apart. Luckily, my grandfather, her father, was able to get her a job as a military doctor. She applied just in time and was employed consistently from then on, even if she wasn't always paid on time.

My father had a different experience. He was a psychiatrist, and there was no money for psychiatric care in post-Soviet Georgia. Once his job went away, he became an entrepreneur and launched the import-and-export business, and a currency exchange, and tried manufacturing different products. He was very creative and tried everything he could think of to make money, but whenever he made any progress with one of his ventures, he was hit with the reality of doing business in Georgia. There was no law. It was just like dealing with the Mafia in the United States; in fact, we call it the Mafia here too. If you didn't have money to pay for "protection," there was nothing to stop them from coming and taking everything away. And they did.

The amazing thing is that all the projects my father tried to get started ten or fifteen years ago are big businesses in Georgia today. His former partner in the medicine importing business is now the owner of one of the big pharmaceutical companies in Georgia, along with a hospital chain and a pharmacy chain. The Georgian spring water he was bottling and exporting to Russia is now a big business … owned by Russians. But for all his brilliant business ideas, my father got nothing. Whatever he developed, someone more powerful came along and took it from him.

This had serious, real-life consequences for my family. By 2001, we could no longer afford our apartment. Since my mother's father had died, we sold our home, and my mother, brother, and I moved to the apartment in the central city where I had lived as a little girl. I still went to the Italian school in my old neighborhood. I still went to Italy every year. And our Italian host families still came back to visit, but they would stay at my grandmother's house. My mother, brother, and I would all move into my grandmother's room. My brother would sleep on the couch, and the three of us would share the big bed.

My father did not move to my grandmother's house. Instead, he moved to Russia. He couldn't face the shame of being unemployed and living under his wife's parents' roof, so he went to Moscow, hoping he could find work as a doctor there. He wound up doing odd, dirty, menial jobs around the hospital and driving a taxi. He was gone for a long time, sending money every month. Sometimes it was $100, sometimes as much as $250. I would much rather have had my father with me. I missed him terribly.

Anyway, now you probably understand why I didn't want to become a doctor. If I wanted the peace and freedom I saw in Italy, I knew that whatever career I chose, I needed to make money.

Growing up in a country with so little, I guess I always had money on my mind. As a little girl, I would make homemade crafts and pieces of jewelry and sell them at school or out in the streets. Sometimes people who were passing by would just give me money and not take anything because I was a cute little girl selling stuff. I would put on plays with my friends and charge for tickets.

I was also clever. When I wrote those legal cases for my grandfather, he paid me by the page, so I had the genius idea of writing in really big letters. That way, instead of ten pages, I was able to charge him for fifty pages to write the same information. My grandfather didn't confront me about this scheme, probably because he thought it was savvy and funny. However, he did eventually realize that paying by the page was not the best idea because he would go bankrupt.

I was aware of money and the things it could do, but I also knew that in my country, the value of currency was not stable. Money in Georgia frequently lost its value—you would be able to afford something one week but not the next. So I devised a system for dealing with my finances that took this into account. I knew I wanted to always have a cushion, because you never know what will happen in the future, even if what I saved lost some of its value. I also knew that if I wanted something really, really badly, which would make me happy in the moment, I should buy it and get it (and, more likely, eat it), because I might not be able to afford it in a week. I ended up with a 40/60 ratio—I saved 40 percent of whatever I earned and spent 60 percent on the things I wanted.

***

In my tenth year of school, one of my teachers in Georgia gave me a job opportunity. A Georgian TV channel was going to air a popular Italian cop show, and they needed someone to translate the scripts from Italian to Georgian. My teacher had been offered the job herself, but she saw it as a good opportunity for a student and asked if there were any volunteers. I was, of course, that volunteer. It was a win-win for me and for the TV channel. They were able to pay me less, since I was not an adult or a professional translator, and I could make money doing a fun, interesting job. It really was both of those things—doing the job right meant going beyond literally making the translations and understanding the humor in Italian, so I could replicate it with the Georgian version of the joke. My supervisors greatly appreciated how I took the time to figure out what would be funny to their Georgian audience. They asked me to continue in my eleventh (and final) year of school, but I had to stop. If I was going to have the future I wanted, that I had been working so hard for, I had one job left. I needed to pass the exam to get into the university that would set me on that path. My final year of school would be spent preparing for that exam.

At first, I was not even sure which exam I would be taking. Students in Georgia and the post-Soviet world in general must pass an exam specific to the thing they want to study and then attend a university that specializes in that subject area. Since I didn't know what I wanted to do, I didn't know which university I should go to, so I studied every subject as if that would be my choice.

This exam process was part of the reason my parents wanted me to study medicine. They knew they could help me navigate the system and pass the test to get into the right university, which was challenging in a system that was chaotic and corrupt. Sometimes you could pass a test and lose your spot in the university, because someone else bribed someone in power for it. But like my grandfather, my parents ultimately trusted me to make my own decision about what my future would be. And after everything they had been through just trying to survive, I was focused on a career that could help make life better for all of us. If money was the key to freedom, and to the kind of secure future I wanted, I wanted to be able to earn enough for my entire family. After all, they had given everything to me, including this freedom to choose my own path. So I needed to choose carefully.

My grandfather offered me the best guidance. He encouraged me to think about what I might want to do for the whole of my life and what opportunities were in the marketplace. That meant listening to my heart but, at the same time, being rational about what would enable me to survive and get through life in the kinds of circumstances we experienced in Georgia. As much as I loved acting and dancing, those were not well-paid careers in Georgia, so I gave those things up when I turned fifteen to focus exclusively on my studies.

I had a vague idea of what I wanted to do, based at least in part on what I had seen my father go through as an entrepreneur. I wanted to be a corporate lawyer, so I could help bring some rules and stability to our economic systems. There was a knowledge gap in my country that resulted in none of our institutions in this area working in a proper way. I felt like this career would utilize what I had learned about the law from my grandfather as well as my math skills. But there was no university I could find where I could prepare for a career in corporate law.

However, there was a fairly new and very well-regarded university in my area that addressed another huge gap in my country—business administration. No one in Georgia knew anything about marketing, or finances, or "management style." Nothing was transparent, and financial reports were not in line with any standards. I realized this new profession would be very important to my country over the next decade as we continued to grow and develop, and fit the same skill set I would need for corporate law.

I changed my mind about being a lawyer and set my sights on this university.

My parents were worried about this decision. Not only was there nothing they could do to help me, but this also was not a state university; it had just become 100 percent private, and their acceptance policy was very new and very strict. You had to pass the entrance exam, which was normal, but you also had to fill out an application, like in the United States, and pass exams in both Georgian and in English. And the school wasn't just selective, but it was also expensive—far too expensive for my parents. My father could not even afford to live in the same country as his family! But I had my heart set on this new "Harvard of the Caucasus." I promised my parents that if they could somehow come up with the money to pay for my first semester, I would do well enough that they would not have to pay for anything else. And if I failed, I could also transfer to any of the state universities.

They agreed to let me try. My next challenge was to get in.

Being the Harvard of the Caucasus, this new school attracted a lot of children from very rich and powerful families. These kids wore Gucci and Versace and talked about cars and perfume and stuff that was really nonsense for me. The only problem was these students were now my competition, and they would have extra help preparing for their entrance exams. Their parents could send them to preparatory school, where they would take a year of classes designed to get them ready to take and pass their entrance exams.

I could never ask my parents for more money on top of asking them to pay for my first semester of university. I might as well have asked for the moon. However, I had been saving 40 percent of all the money I had earned for years and years. And in that account, I had just enough money saved to pay for the preparatory school myself. My determination was unshakable. To even get into this preparatory school, I'd spent my summer months staying with my grandparents and studying very hard. My lovely neighbors next door in the country found me a math teacher in the administrative center of my village. My grandfather took me to her home twice a week, where she gave me prepared simulations of the entrance exam. Reviewing my results, I continued to work on errors again and again. And across the other subjects, I did the same by myself.

Once I was in, that whole last year before university was a walk through hell. I would eat one meal in the morning and go to the Italian school until five at night. Then I would cross town to start my test preparatory school at seven. That ended at ten, so I would go home and study my lessons from both schools until three or four in the morning. Then I would get up an hour or two later and do it all over again.

I was totally, utterly, completely exhausted. My parents told me to slow down, that it was bad for my health. But I knew that I would not be accepted to the university I wanted to attend without preparation. Everything I had done throughout my childhood to get ready for this moment—the nights spent studying and working and not dating or having fun—would be for nothing. So I kept going. I took the exam and was accepted to the University of the Caucasus with the highest grades.

I would soon find out that karma is a bitch.

Chapter 4

THE BEST-LAID PLANS

One day, when I was still going to the Italian school, I stopped by our cell-phone provider's office on my way home to get the phone my mother and I shared unblocked. A man in his midtwenties who said he worked for the provider approached me in the queue and offered to help. He wrote down my number and spoke to the person at the desk, and they unblocked the phone. I didn't even have to pay anything! I said thank you and went on my way.

Not long afterward, my mother and I started getting strange messages on that phone. She asked me what they were all about. I had no idea. Then I started getting the sense that I was being followed. Every day, the same black BMW was behind the bus I took home from school, turning whenever we turned.

At that time, Georgia was a dangerous place for young women. You could be kidnapped off the street in broad daylight, and if, God forbid, you were raped, you were expected to marry your rapist. Once a man takes your virginity in a strict, patriarchal country like Georgia, you are no longer a virgin and therefore no longer considered "marriage material." Once girls lost their virginity, it was easier to stick with whichever man took it than face the future as an unmarried nonvirgin.

I started getting off the bus earlier, taking different routes home, trying to find places to walk where a car could not follow me. Then one day, I came out of school, and the black BMW was parked by the bus stop. The driver got out.

It was the man from the cell-phone store.

He walked toward me and asked if I remembered him, explaining that he was the stranger who had been sending me messages, that he had pretended to work at the store so he could get at my phone, and that he had been using my number to track me wherever I went, from cell tower to cell tower. He complimented me, saying I was "not like the others" because I was smart and noticed him following me. But he also said that would not help me. I could let him accompany me home or not, but he would always know where I was. One way or another, he was going to make me his.

I jumped on the first bus I saw, even though it was the wrong one, hurried home, and told my mother. My father was in Russia, so she told my aunt, who was the mother of my big, strong, older male cousin, who was more than capable of handling this sort of situation. A little later, I received a very polite message from the man from the cell-phone store apologizing for any discomfort he might have caused me. He never bothered me again.

Unfortunately, not every man in Georgia scares away that easily.

***

I started studying at the University of the Caucasus at age seventeen. With my parents' and grandparents' help, I had laid a foundation for the kind of life I dreamed about when I was in Italy. Now it was time to build it. My university offered an exchange program with Georgia

State University in the United States, and while I had not planned to study across an ocean, this was now a real, attainable goal. All I had to do was continue to do what I had always done—work hard.

The university was only six years old, founded with help from a grant from the US government to provide a Western-style education for the generation that would be running Georgia's economy. Market-based economics was a new concept in my part of the world, so everything at this university was a departure from the way things had always been done. The dean of the school, Kakha Shengelia, who is now a good friend, understood the challenges Georgia faced. He knew that if the people running our economy did not have the same educational foundation as the rest of the world, we would not be able to compete at their level. So he brought a Western-style university program to my country, earning himself the nickname "the Joker of Georgian Education."

At the time, his ideas were considered radical. In the post-Soviet world, a university is typically dedicated only to the students' career track. If you're studying to become an engineer, you go to an engineering university, where all your classes are related to engineering. If you're studying to become a doctor, all your classes are about medicine. But at my university, the first year was devoted to "general education." That meant we had to study everything, including subjects a lot of my classmates had never studied at all. Even though many of them came from wealthy families and had every advantage (which is possibly why they gravitated to business school in the first place), the collapse of the Soviet Union had decimated the Georgian public school system, so students never learned about history or psychology or read great books from around the globe. But because I was educated at the Italian school, I already knew a lot of what was being taught. My first year of university was actually easy—especially compared to what I had gone through the year before to get into my university. Still, I could only relax a little. I needed to stay at the top of my class so I would qualify for scholarships and my tuition would be free. That way I could keep my promise to my parents, and of course achieve my dream of studying abroad.

A week or so into the first semester, my university held a "team-building" challenge to help all the new students get to know each other. It was another novel Western idea, modeled after the activities corporations do to help their employees learn to work together in a fun, informal setting. We all met at a city park where there was a mountain, and our job was to work in teams to get to the top of this mountain without any sort of transportation. We were given the first piece of a map to our destination, where we would solve a challenge and get our next clue.

Right away, I noticed a tall, handsome boy with hair the color of corn and deep-blue eyes, showing off. He was doing everything a person could possibly do to get my attention, offering me his help one minute, teasing me the next, always making a big show of competing in each challenge. I had never met anyone so self-confident. Of course, he was the first to reach the top of the mountain and win the prize, at which point he asked me for my phone number. I told him no.

Later that day, my mother said I had a call on our landline. A male voice identified himself. I didn't recognize the name.

"The winner," he reminded me.

It was the cocky boy from the team-building contest, who apparently had been trying to meet me since before the mountain challenge. He explained how he first saw me when he walked into the wrong class the first week of school. I remembered the teacher yelling at him to leave. He remembered me as "an angel sitting in the front row." After that, he asked the professors to put us on the same team for the contest. When I would not give him my phone number, he went through the school records to find my information and then had a friend who worked for the phone company help him find my home phone number, which is easy to do when you live in a country without privacy laws.

I couldn't help being impressed by how hard this boy worked just to talk to me. But I was not interested in dating him. I had promised my father that I would avoid relationships until I finished my education. He wanted me to realize my dreams, not put all my time and energy into helping some other person realize their dreams—and he understood the mentality of Georgian men, who wanted good-looking wives that they would treat like slaves who would cook and clean and take care of them. Even though Georgians typically marry young, my parents had waited to marry until they finished their education. I did not want to disappoint my father, and I also agreed with him. So I told the boy we could only be friends.

His concept of "friendship" meant phoning me multiple times a day, waiting for me outside my classes, walking me home, and making it clear that he was in love with me and he would not be happy until I was also in love with him. I learned his life story—that he came from a wealthy family, that he had lived in the United States and graduated from high school there, and that his father hanged himself when he was only a boy. That gave his story this extra touch of drama and tragedy, plus he was brilliant and confident and handsome and everything a girl would want in a boyfriend. But I did not want a boyfriend. I was only seventeen. I was still a virgin. I had never even kissed a boy.

Because he was constantly calling and coming to our apartment, my mother and grandmother got to know this boy, and they were not as impressed as I was. As a neurologist (and the wife of a psychiatrist), my mother understands human behavior, and the way this boy behaved worried her. So she asked around. Tbilisi is a small city, and soon she knew about his family situation and his father. She heard rumors that he also had psychological problems, had gotten involved with drugs in America, and had to come home because he was not stable enough to go to university in the United States. They were just rumors, she knew, but they seemed to indicate a pattern that fit with his obsession with me.

I had never, ever lied to my parents. I had never even hidden anything from them. But I knew I could not tell my mother everything about this boy—because some of the things he did were too upsetting to share. I didn't tell her how he constantly put pressure on me to be his girlfriend, or that he spread rumors that I actually was his girlfriend, and even that I secretly had his baby, to keep the other boys who were interested in me away. I didn't tell her how he threatened those other boys when they got near me and sometimes threatened to hurt himself if I dated someone else.

But most of the time, he did other things—things that, of course, would impress a young girl who had never been in a relationship with anyone before. There were so many flowers, thousands of them, with letters inside for me to read. They would come every day, to the point where I would wait for my roses to arrive. He would give me gifts of clothing that just happened to be my size. Late one night, he called me to look out the window, and I saw a big heart with my name written inside in fire. It was all so romantic, having this brilliant, handsome boy so obviously in love with me. Every single day, he would wait under my balcony in his car, just to show me he was always nearby. He used to throw tiny pebbles at my window, and I would look out to see the candles, the flowers, and the messages written on the ground. The fact that my mother didn't like him made it feel even more romantic, if that was even possible.

He spent so much time and energy on me that he started struggling in school. He had a Western education like I did and was so brilliant he could listen to a lecture once and pass the test, without ever taking a note or studying. But he was missing his lectures entirely because he was walking me home, or buying me presents, or making sure no other boy could get close to me. I felt like I was swept up in a whirlwind, so mixed up and emotional and confused. I felt excited and guilty at the same time. Even more, I felt loved. In my seventeen-year-old mind, love was supposed to be painful. I felt like we were Romeo and Juliet, suffering for our forbidden love.

After a while, I started wondering, Why shouldn't I open myself up to a relationship? I knew I was a strong enough student, and dedicated enough, that my studies wouldn't suffer. If he knew I belonged to him, maybe he would be able to focus on his studies, too, and everything would be OK. Maybe even better than OK. We were both smart students at a top school who had lived abroad and wanted (I thought) similar things out of life. Plus, he was nice to look at. We made a good couple.

I knew I could not hide this from my parents, so at the beginning of my second year of university, I told my mother I was considering dating this boy. For the last time, she told me exactly how she felt. She explained that she did not think that he was the right person for me or that he would make me happy. I told her I didn't care, that I loved him and that was all that mattered. So she told me that if I insisted on dating him, to please do only that and not let him pull me away from my studies and my future plans. I agreed. Of course I wouldn't let a boy destroy my dreams!

She never mentioned it again.

I told the boy, "OK, let's be in a relationship with each other. Maybe something good will happen."

I always knew, on some level, it was a very bad idea. I did not know it was the beginning of my own personal blitz, which would wipe away everything I had worked so hard to build.

***

From that day on, I was torn between two fires—the fire of my love for my parents and wanting to be the good girl they had known and raised, and love for this boy who seemed to be so in love with me. His mother invited me to their home to get acquainted, and I was impressed by the huge apartment on the twelfth floor in the central part of the city where only three people were living: my boyfriend, his little brother, and his mother. His mother was very nice and supportive of me, probably because she loved my boyfriend very much and wanted her son to be happy. She was beautiful and nice and educated and seemed more like a friend to him than a mother, doing everything for him and supporting his decisions. She was very unlike my mother, who did not approve of mine.

Now that we were officially boyfriend and girlfriend, my boyfriend marked his territory all around me like a dog, parading me around school like a prize. Everyone knew we were together, but somehow, he was even more obsessive and possessive than before. "You are very beautiful," he would tell me. "You are nice, you are a good student … I don't know when you are going to leave me." He continued to question my commitment to him, especially when I studied with groups that included other boys. He asked me not to do that, to study alone at home. Soon, he decided there was one brilliant solution, one thing that would solve all our problems and enable him to focus and do his work and not worry about me all the time.

I should marry him.

If we made it legal and official that I belonged to him, and everyone knew it, he would not have to worry. He would finish his studies and help me finish university, and we could have the lives and careers we planned.

I loved my boyfriend, but I did not want to get married. I had never even kissed him!

But I was falling in love with him, because it was impossible to resist him, and late that autumn, I finally admitted it to him. To me, that was the most solemn promise I had ever made. I considered myself bound to him forever. He was walking me home, and when we were three hundred meters from my apartment, he suddenly said, "Don't walk around the corner. Close your eyes, and you will see I have a surprise for you." I closed my eyes, expecting some sort of present or note like he usually gave me.

And he kissed me.

I felt a million things at once—angry that he deceived me, because that was not the way I imagined my first kiss would be, but also, something different … like warmth going through my veins. And underneath it all, this knowing that something was wrong. Everything was happening so fast, it all felt out of control. But I pushed those thoughts away and focused on the feeling of being in love and the future we would build together.

I had big dreams for my future. I wanted to be independent. Well, first I wanted to be free from wondering how I would survive the next day, things like how I would get money for the bus and my books and the Xerox machine. But beyond that, I wanted independence, which to me meant free choice—the ability to do what I wanted to do and not what I was obliged to do. I wanted my own home without any parents or grandparents or siblings around, as much as I loved them. For that to happen, I needed to do well in my studies, graduate from one of the American universities, and ideally get my MBA there.

But now that I had committed my heart to my boyfriend, he had to be incorporated into my plans. And at that moment, he was not holding up his end of the bargain. He was constantly in danger of failing out of the university that was supposed to make everything possible. I was on the phone with him every night, helping him with philosophy, history, math, all the classes where his grades weren't high enough. He didn't care; he said the only thing he cared about was marrying me. Once he achieved that, he promised he would finish university and find a job and live a good life. But until he was living with me, he would not be able to do those things, because all he could think about was me.

***

During the second semester of my second year of university, a group of Georgia's biggest banks and private companies held a job fair for university students. I submitted my CV to several companies that I had researched and thought offered good opportunities, one of which was the Bank of Georgia. They were launching a new internship program where they would employ university students, train them in a range of different roles at the bank, and prepare them to become good, loyal employees in the future. It was an exciting time at the bank—they were rebranding to serve our new economy and launching a lot of innovative new products, which was exactly the kind of work I wanted to be doing, helping build a strong financial system so Georgia would grow and thrive. I set my sights on that internship.

After first passing a test to qualify, the twenty or so interns in the class went through several rounds of training in all the different products the bank offered, with exams we needed to pass on each. The group continued to narrow until there were only a handful of us left. We were asked to present a case study before a panel representing bank management, and the panel would then decide who would move up into the bank's paid training program. I must have done this case study perfectly because even now, when I meet the people who first hired me, they remember me as the smiling girl with the braids who had all those innovative ideas.

I was hired to do on-the-job training all around the bank, so I rotated from one department to another, from logistics to credit risk to corporate banking to treasury to law. This gave me a holistic understanding of how the system was working. I knew everyone everywhere at the bank and developed strong relationships with colleagues and clients that helped me to do things faster and better. It was an incredible opportunity, and I was very grateful. But it was also a lot of work, and at first, the work was unpaid. That meant walking to my trainings instead of taking the bus to save money, which meant I had no time to study except while I was walking, which meant I occasionally fell and hurt my knee or crashed into a tree.

Work and school were the best parts of my life. Which was good, because it was becoming clear I would probably be finishing my education in Tbilisi and not at Georgia State University in the United States, or even a university in Europe. It was obvious my boyfriend was never going to let me go. He could not stand to have me out of his sight for an hour; he was jealous even when I was studying, interrupting and making scenes when I had group projects. He told me that if I loved him, I wouldn't do things that made him jealous, like spend time with my friends, that I should be obedient and do my homework alone. I felt like a prisoner, but I also felt that his distress and pain were proof of how much he loved me. He loved me so much, he failed our second year at university and learned he would have to transfer to another school.

I decided I had to marry him. It was the only way to keep him from destroying himself.

Chapter 5

HERE COMES THE BRIDE

There are two kinds of marriage that are recognized as legal in Georgia. Civil marriage is similar to being married by a judge in the United States. There is a ceremony performed by a civil official or the Georgian government, and the marriage is entered into the public record. There is no law preventing divorce in Georgia, so Georgians can get married and divorced as many times as they want.

Marriage in the Orthodox Christian Church, when you pledge your vows to each other in front of God, is also recognized as legal by the Georgian government. But once you are married in the Orthodox Christian Church, you can only marry once. It's not that you can't choose to divorce and even remarry—you absolutely can, but with the understanding that you are committing a mortal sin in the eyes of God. The church does allow some second marriages, but only with a special permit and only after proving grave grounds. Basically, when you marry in the Orthodox Church, if you take your vows seriously, you really are pledging yourself to another person until death.

I saw that as a solution to my problem.

My boyfriend knew how deeply I believed in God, and that I had integrity and cared very much about keeping my promises. If I were to marry him in the church, he would not be able to question my commitment. He would know I was his, so he would be able to breathe, and he would let me breathe, and we could get on with our lives. I approached him with what I thought was the perfect plan; we would marry in the Church, but we would do it secretly. We would not tell my family. I would continue living in my grandmother's apartment until we finished our studies. Then we would declare everything to our parents and get married under civil law with all our families and friends and begin our official lives together as husband and wife.

He said yes.

I had never lied to my parents before, but I saw no other choice. And so, just like Romeo and Juliet, we got secretly married. He swore before the icon of the mother of God that he would keep his word, honoring that promise we made to each other—a promise he would later break. But there we were, holding a ceremony in the church, with two of his friends and one of mine as our witnesses. Then we went to a small restaurant to celebrate. After that, I went home and continued my normal life, just like we had planned.

It was only a few days before my husband was unhappy again. If I was really his wife, why had I only kissed him and nothing more? Was I lying about loving him? Was I not really his wife at all? He was always jealous, always suspicious, just like before. One day when his mother was away and he was home alone, he invited me to his house, and I gave him my virginity, hoping adding that element to our marriage would prove to my secret husband that I belonged to him. I went on birth control right after that. There was no way I was going to have a baby. That would ruin everything.

A few months later, it was winter, and my mother was in bed with a terrible case of influenza. She was lying in bed with an oxygen mask, and I was lying with her, giving her medicine and trying to cheer her up, when my phone rang. It was my husband, angry that, the day before, I had worked with a study group that included a male student who was attracted to me. My husband started yelling and accusing me like he always did, but my mother was so sick. I was really worried about her. So I told him we could talk about it later.

He sent a picture of our marriage certificate to my mother's cell phone.

While she was processing that piece of information, he called her. "My wife is not living with me because she's afraid of your opinion," he said. "Your daughter is not a virgin anymore, so what are you afraid of? Let her come live with me."

It was the worst moment of my life.

My mother, still on oxygen, called my father in Moscow and told him. He said he would come home as soon as he could, which meant giving up his ability to work in Moscow and send home money, because he had been in Russia illegally. Once he crossed the border, he would not be able to go back. Everything was falling apart, everyone was upset, and it was all my fault. I was so ashamed and embarrassed and sad; I had let my parents down, I had lied, and I still loved and missed my husband, whom I was not allowed to see. My family put me on lockdown until my father got home, only letting me out to go to and from school, always accompanied. Other than that, I spent the whole week in my room, crying. I felt like no one would ever forgive me—not that I deserved their forgiveness.

Then my father arrived and immediately set up a meeting with my husband's family. My mother-in-law and my husband's uncle came to our home, and everyone sat together and talked everything out. My husband's uncle promised to treat me as his own child and pay for everything we needed to get through university and start our lives together. My husband and I explained how much we loved each other, and that we were going to stay in school and get our degrees and live good lives. In the end, everyone gave us their blessing, and my husband officially asked my parents for my hand in marriage.

My father asked me if I really loved my husband, and I told him I did. He said that if this was what I really wanted for my future, there was nothing he could or would do to stop me. From then on, everyone was supportive, even my grandfather Konstantine, who had such big dreams for me. He said that if I was happy (and since I was not going to give up my studies), it was OK with him.

The summer before our last year of university was a happy time. We planned our civil wedding and traveled around, seeing family and celebrating our engagement. We took a honeymoon trip to Turkey, and my husband told me he'd pay for me to go to university there and get my MBA. When we got back to Georgia, I relocated from my parents' home to my husband's mother's home up on the twelfth floor. It was so big, much larger and more comfortable than my grandmother's apartment, but there were only four of us: me, my husband, his mother, and his little brother, whom I loved. Everything was financed by my husband's uncle, who was a successful businessman with no wife and no children. My mother-in-law did not work.

We planned our wedding for September, three days before our fourth year of university was set to start. On the ninth of September, we had our official, not-very-huge-but-also-not-very-small wedding in a beautiful venue filled with flowers. All our friends and relatives were there. I wore a beautiful white dress. I looked amazing.

I was nineteen.

Two days later, on the eleventh of September, I was driving back and forth between my parents' home and husband's home with our wedding presents, and my husband did not come home on time. He was very late, long past when he should have arrived, so I started calling him but was unable to reach him. As it got later, his mother started to worry and started looking for him, calling him, calling his friends. No one knew where he was or what was going on.

I was at my parents' apartment when my husband suddenly pulled into the driveway in his mother's car (he had no license at this time). He came up all covered in blood, and since my parents are doctors, they immediately started examining him. Was he hurt? Had he been in a car accident? Had he fallen? They realized he was healthy and sound, but he was also very nervous. He explained what had happened, all in a rush. He had gotten a call from a friend who had been in our wedding party. He and his brother had been robbed, and his brother was stabbed during the fight and was bleeding. They needed my husband to take him to the hospital right away. They were worried that if he didn't hurry, his friend would die.

My husband jumped into the car and drove to where the fight had happened. When he got there, it was still going on, like a riot—everyone was hitting each other. His friend was lying half dead on the ground, but in order to reach him, he had to first get through the fight. He managed to grab the knife from the attacker who had stabbed his friend, and after a struggle, he stabbed the attacker in the leg to get him to let go. Then my husband was able to grab his friend and hoist him onto his shoulders, get him in the car, and take him to the hospital. The doctors said it was a miracle. If my husband had waited even an additional ten minutes, his friend would have died from the loss of blood. When my father saw the car, he couldn't believe how much blood there was.

They were lucky. But the attacker my husband stabbed was not. His friends all ran away from the scene and left him to bleed to death on the street.

To accidentally kill someone in self-defense is scary anywhere, but it was especially scary at that time in Georgia, where there was still no real or consistent law. The family of the friend my husband saved was not willing to get involved to help clear his name. So it was decided that, two days after our wedding, my husband should go into hiding until the police finished their investigation, when they hopefully would find he did nothing wrong. Otherwise, he would have been put in prison right away, and at that time in Georgia, prison was a real hell. There were no real rules and no system, so you could be murdered or wind up addicted to something against your will. There was not enough food, and any food you'd get there was inedible. Everything was full of rats, of dust, of mud. And in the rooms designed to hold four prisoners, there were twenty.

We all knew my husband would probably have to go to jail eventually. But until we could figure things out a little more clearly and make a plea bargain, we decided the best thing for him was to hide. So he went into hiding, which left his mother so distraught she kicked me out of the house. She said I should not be living there if her son was not. I would have gone home to my parents, but one of my husband's relatives was smart enough to see that my mother-in-law was making a mistake. If I went home, I might stay there forever. He offered to let me stay at his home while my husband was hiding in the mountains, and he and his family were lovely—they drove me to the university and back home every day, they fed me, they took care of me. I will be forever grateful to them.

My husband moved from place to place to evade the police, only seeing me or his family occasionally, and always in secret. The process was stressful, especially for a young man who was not very mentally strong to begin with. Then one day, the police followed my mother-in-law and discovered where he was hiding, and he was caught and put in jail. He said he could not have remained in hiding much longer anyway or he would have gone crazy.

Since his friend's family refused to testify to help him, my husband's best option was to admit guilt to a lesser charge. He wound up sentenced to six years in prison, at the age of twenty. He had only one year left before he would have received his university degree.

Chapter 6

THE PRISONER'S WIFE

I missed my husband desperately, and he missed me. I wrote him letters in prison, and he asked me to write them long, as these letters helped him to kill the time. I used to incorporate my poems, too, and the letters would be as long as fifteen to twenty pages, describing my aspirations, plans, activities, and my feelings about him and the situation I had to go through. Later he told me that everyone in the jail got jealous when he received letters from me. When he got out, the only thing he took home from prison were those thousands of pages of letters. I always wanted to combine them together as a book.

While my husband was in jail, I was able to finish my final year at university, even though he had discouraged me from doing so. When I graduated, I'd been given two diplomas: one was the legal document, an ordinary size, and the other was the beautiful, big, framed diploma with fine script stating that I, Tamar Gakharia, had graduated with distinction, as well as a university seal and the signatures of the dean and university president. I hung it in the bedroom, and looking at it each night, I felt proud of myself. It was like a symbol of the first victory or a trophy that I was able to get in return for overcoming another blitz.

But when he came out of jail and saw the diploma, he tore it from the wall and hit me over my head with it, yelling that I did not listen to him and did not obey his directive to stay at home. He was furious that I'd deviated from his pleas: while he'd been suffering in jail, my accomplishments were just more cause for jealousy.

Shards of broken glass got stuck in my neck, my shoulders, and my feet. I was unable to remove one of them from my foot; it remains there today, like a message from the past, reminding me: no matter what happens, women should not give up on getting an education and pursuing their dreams.

And that commitment paid off. The bank hired me for a paid position very quickly out of the 2006 internship program—then in 2007, because I was still in my last year of university, I started half time in the bank headquarters. I did so well there that I was offered a transfer to the corporate department. I graduated first in the entire faculty rankings at the university and began my full-time job as a corporate service manager, where I continued to excel. By age twenty-one, I was in charge of all the bank's credit products, all the banking products and services for corporate clients, completing credit and financial analyses, preparing financial statements and reports, selling products, servicing clients, monitoring projects and documentary operations, negotiating and drafting agreements, and doing more.

With my husband locked away in prison, work became the thing that saved me, that gave my life purpose. I loved being able to look at my country through the prism of developed economies around the world and see where the gaps were. At school, my favorite classes were the ones with case studies that demonstrated the failures and successes of famous global companies. It was exciting to see how these businesses everyone had heard of experienced the same issues I was learning about at school and at my job. I think both experiences worked together holistically to give me an incredible education and a strong foundation for a successful career.

But our new nation's foundation was in danger. In the summer of 2008, tensions escalated in the South Ossetia region of the country. South Ossetian separatists who were backed by Russia began targeting Georgian villages in the area, peppering them with artillery shells. Property was destroyed, and many villagers and young, barely trained Georgian "peacekeeping" forces were killed. One hundred miles away in Tbilisi, we went to work every day, as if nothing was happening. This was normal—if we stopped working every time Russia threatened our country, we would never get anything done. But we weren't really getting anything done beyond showing up for work. The climate was so volatile, the bank was afraid to take any risks, and that meant no new business.

I remember sitting in my chair, waiting to present a project to the credit committee for approval, watching each person who entered to present something before me get rejected. I realized my client and their project probably faced the same fate. I was a huge champion of this client—they were a telecommunication service and equipment supplier, one of the biggest in Georgia, part of the new wave of private businesses laying the bricks toward building a new, modern Georgia. Financing their project was not only important for their company, but it was also important for the whole country.

My mind scrolled through all the possible questions the credit committee might have for me, and how I might answer so I didn't get rejected. I was so nervous my palms were sweating. But when it was finally my turn, the committee did not have any questions to ask me. They had already decided to say no.

This was not an acceptable outcome for me.

I started talking. I told them they were making a mistake. I explained why it was important, even in that moment of turmoil—

especially in that moment of turmoil—to invest in this client. I told them this client was part of the fight for Georgia, as telecommunication was (and is) a highly strategic area for the country and the project the client was pursuing was clearly the most advanced step in developing this striving sector—a sector that would, in turn, make our country better, stronger, and more independent.

And, amazingly, the credit committee actually listened to me. We discussed all the possible outcomes, including what would happen if the company went bankrupt, or if the country itself failed. We analyzed all the pros and cons. And in the end, they gave me the OK to finance the project.

Just then, the secretary, who was not allowed inside the committee meeting, rushed into the room. She had been calling and calling, but no one put her through, and there was an emergency. Russian tanks had invaded Gori, a city only thirty kilometers away from Tbilisi. We were at war.

I took all the signed papers, so there would be no way for the committee to go back on their decision. Then I sent a message to my client that his credit was approved.

He called back and said, "Are you crazy? Are you working on my project while we're surrounded by Russian troops?"

Outside the office, everything was turmoil. Cars were lined up for miles at the borders with Azerbaijan and Armenia as people tried to flee. I am proud to say my family was not among them. As a high-ranking military doctor, my mother couldn't leave the country because she was called into the field to help. My father, of course, refused to leave without her, but he would have stayed to protect his country to his last breath regardless. The same was true of all the men in my family, including my brother and my husband's brother. It was also true for me.

The hard part was, we had no idea where my mother was. We called and left message after message, but there was no reply for days. We had no way of knowing her location or if she was even alive. We also had no idea what would happen to my husband in prison, especially if Russian tanks were about to overrun our city and reclaim our country.

On August 12, 2008, I went to a huge rally in the center of Tbilisi, joining 150,000 to 200,000 of my fellow Georgians to demand our freedom. A string of leaders from Eastern Europe took the stage to express solidarity with Georgia. The presidents of Poland, Ukraine, Estonia, Latvia, and Lithuania all joined our president, Mikheil Saakashvili, on stage, delivering speeches condemning Russia and promising to stand with us. Nicolas Sarkozy, then the president of France, was not at the rally—he was busy traveling between Tbilisi and Moscow, negotiating a ceasefire.

And then, after three days, it was all over. Georgia had lost 20 percent of its territory and thousands of people were made refugees, but we remained a sovereign nation.

When we finally spoke to my mother, it had been three days since we last talked to her. She had been unable to communicate because she was hiding her location near the front line, at the military hospital in Gori. She coordinated the medical team's efforts and treated villagers who tried to fight off Russian tanks and bombs with axes and farm equipment. She told me the hospital where she was working was like "a sea of dead people."

When I went back to work, the project I pitched for my telecommunications client the day of the Russian invasion went forward and was a huge success. I still have a good relationship with that client and his organization, which is now multinational. I actually made an impact.

Unfortunately, the war took a terrible toll on my grandfather Konstantine. He had been traumatized by the first civil war in the '90s—he fought the gangs that robbed the villages, and he himself was robbed five or six times, to the point where, when gangsters approached his house the seventh time, he went after them with an axe. They had already taken all his hunting guns, despite their being officially registered. He spent the last decades of his life defending the people in his village from criminals like these, but, when it happened again in 2008, he was an old man. There was no fight left in him.

He was sitting on the balcony, smoking his pipe, when my grandmother saw him fall. He had a stroke, and since it was not possible to get help to the countryside in time to stop it from doing damage, he became paralyzed, only able to move his head and his hands. My grandmother, who was also elderly and not in the best health, had to look after him. Every day, she would massage him, roll him back, change him, and keep him clean and give him his treatments for his diabetes. This went on for years, until she, too, had a stroke. Then they were both lying in bed side by side. My father hired nurses to look after them and went to see them as often as he could.

***

By this time, I was living in my husband's apartment again. When he went to jail, he asked his mother to take me back so she could keep an eye on me and make sure I did not wind up back with my parents. We did not know if he would be in prison for four years or twelve years, or anywhere in between. There was no consistent law we could rely on, so we went back and forth with the prosecutors and the lawyers, spending more and more money in hopes of negotiating something that would get him home. My husband was a brilliant student with a clean record, he had only killed his victim in self-defense, so we hoped we could get him a pardon, or at least a sentence of only a year or two.

While he waited in prison, he continued to manipulate me psychologically. He wrote me letters and texted and called me from different cell phones—one of the perks of having prisons with no rules is that if you have the money, you can have your own cell phone in prison. So my husband was able to continually make demands. He wanted me to stay home and not to go to work, not to go to school, not to do anything until his return. I told him that was impossible, because I was responsible for taking care of both of us. And we always needed more money, for the prosecutors, for the lawyers, for food and protection and phone privileges for my husband in prison. We had already exhausted his uncle's fortune, so there was no money except what I brought in.

As for my dreams, they no longer mattered. The foundation I had laid so carefully for myself, the bricks I honed over years of studying and working so hard, had been lost to the blitz of my love. There would be no MBA from the United States, or even Turkey. If I was honest with myself, I would have known even when he promised me on our honeymoon that he was telling a lie. In some way, I always knew. I just would not admit it to myself at the time. So now, my future plans were simple: work as hard as I possibly could to get money to survive and get my husband out of prison. That was my only goal.

And I did well, maybe because work was the one thing in my life that I could control. It was also the only thing that could give me pleasure. I got real joy from serving my clients and managers and helping them make their dreams come true. And somehow, doing that, I was able to keep a flicker of my own dreams alive. My career became a sort of light at the end of the tunnel. And I kept getting closer, just by focusing on the opportunity I still had in front of me.

It may not have been grad school in the United States, but my work was exciting and challenging. Unlike Western countries, Georgia had no concept of marketing beyond advertising. I had learned about marketing from the motherland of marketing—the United States—and understood things that most people in Georgia had never been exposed to, like studying marketing analytics and how they shape proper product development, assessing demand and supply curves, understanding optimal production levels, and more. These were all things that Georgian businesses would need to succeed but did not understand. I started looking at my country as one big company, looking for the gaps where we needed to build systems to make it operational.

I wound up working with around sixty companies, some of which were very sophisticated and had good systems and were easy to work with, and others that did not know how to manage their accounts because all the systems were so new. We had to educate clients about the products we were selling because they didn't understand what they wanted or needed. We were basically teaching them how to function in a capitalist economy. We taught them about things like earnings before interest, taxes, depreciation, and amortization, and how a proper accounting system works, how they should account for transactions, and how they should present their financial statements.

Some of these companies were still operating in the twentieth century. I'll never forget one experience when I needed to make some inputs for a client, and the only sources of data were the paper receipts from the cash register printer. The papers were all about fifty meters long, so I had to cut them into sheets and use a ladder to attach them to the top of the wall, until the papers covered the room like wallpaper. Every time I entered the bank with those rolls of receipts in my hands, everyone would joke, "Here comes Tamar, with her wallpaper again."

***

In the evening, after work, I went back to my "other life" as a prisoner's wife. After work, I would shop for food for my husband at the open-air market where the local farmers sold their goods, then prepare a meal for him with his mother. We would have to pack it the right way to be accepted at the prison—you had to cut it, slice it, blend it all a certain way for it to be allowed in the jail. Then either she or I would go to the prison and wait in the queues to submit the food, plus cigarettes and whatever other extras we could get for my husband.

Emotionally, socially, even physically, that part of my life was like being in hell. I felt so guilty about what I was doing to my family—in Georgia, everyone knows everyone, so your reputation means everything, and our family had never been connected to any kind of crime. My grandfather had been a lawyer! Now I was the wife of a murderer. I was too ashamed and embarrassed to visit my grandparents' village; I did not want to bother my parents and stress them out with my problems, and between my work hours and study hours, I was not in shape to talk with anybody anyway. So I didn't see anybody. My only goal was to make my husband free. Almost everything I earned went straight to the jail—to bribe the staff to keep him safe, to allow him to bathe more than once every two weeks, to talk with his family more often, to top up his mobile phone, to send him money for cigarettes. I really believed in my heart that, when we could live together again, we would live happily ever after.

His uncle, his mother, and I were constantly negotiating with the lawyers and the prosecutor's office, seeking connections or help to get him home. The people we needed help from, who could offer help, were not providing it. The family of the friend whose life he saved refused to tell the real story. The family of the victim would not consent to lowering the charge. Eventually he was sentenced to six years in jail, which at least gave us a road map of what to do next, which was to continue to negotiate. Everything in Georgia could be bought, but you had to know the right person to buy it from. If you went to the wrong person, you would spend your money for nothing.

For a year and a half, we begged for a lower sentence or, preferably, a plea bargain. My mother even went to the victim's family on my behalf, asking them to at least have mercy on me, his wife, who had done nothing wrong. Because of my mother, the victim's family started to think about the reality of what had happened, and eventually they consented to a deal with the prosecutor's office. But it took us years just to be able to tell the prosecutors the whole truth about what happened, and we were able to only because my mother had intervened.

This was not the only time my mother protected my husband, despite her feelings about him. At one point he was seriously injured— we were told he fell from the upper level of the prison bed, but even now, we don't know if that's true—and wound up with a skull fracture, which could have killed him or left him disabled. Because of her position, my mother was able to get him transferred from the prison hospital to the civil hospital, which probably saved his life.

We were able to visit my husband in the hospital. During that period, the victim's family finally consented, and we were able to come to an agreement with the prosecutor's office. They agreed to take two years off his sentence, lowering it from six years to four—provided we, of course, paid another fine. He was in the hospital recovering for a month and a half before he was brought back to jail, and even then, he was not 100 percent. At some point after that, the jail itself was destroyed, and he was moved to a new, modern facility, with more of the "comforts" of a Western prison. That was where he would serve the remainder of his sentence.

Chapter 7

REUNITED

Today, as I write this, the streets below my office are filled with young people protesting. It has been more than a year since Russia invaded another former Soviet country, Ukraine, and our entire region is coping with the constant threat of winding up on the wrong side of this aggression. Our government has passed a law that some view as bringing us closer to the Russians and further from the West, possibly jeopardizing our plans to join the European Union, leading to the most massive protests since we first gained independence thirty-five years ago. We are in danger of facing another blitz that will wipe away everything we have been working so hard to build, the free society where people can pursue their dreams without fear. Today, everything is in danger of collapsing, while Russia and the West continue to fight to exert their control.

All we want is to be prosperous and free.

***

The day my husband was set to be freed from prison, I could hardly control my excitement. His mother and I went to the new prison together to wait and stood a few hundred meters away from the entrance, by a little guard gate with a wooden arm that let vehicles in and out. Suddenly, I saw the big, electric metal doors that we passed through each time we went to visit my husband start to slide open. I saw a figure coming through those doors, heading out from the building.

It was my husband, walking toward me.

The second I saw him, I was running. I jumped over the little wooden parking gate and headed straight toward him. The guards yelled for me to stop, but I didn't care. I don't think I even heard them yelling. I ran straight to my husband and hugged him as hard as I had ever hugged anyone in my life. Finally, it was over. Finally, we could start our lives together. That night, his mother, his brother, his uncle, my husband, and I all had dinner together for the first time in years in our apartment on the twelfth floor, which we prepared ourselves from all his favorite things. I showed him the diary I had kept in addition to the letters I wrote to him when he was away—describing my everyday activities and numbering the minutes from the day of his imprisonment—reminding him again of how much I loved him and missed him all those years. It was the happy ending I had been waiting for.

Unfortunately, the story of our marriage was just beginning.

Prison had changed my husband. He went in as one person and came out another. I could understand this, and I don't blame him. He had been through hell, including an actual brain injury that still affected him. But the reality was, instead of the brilliant, promising student with the bright future I had fallen in love with, he was a man with a criminal record, a brain injury, and, I would soon learn, a secret drug habit. I, on the other hand, was a university graduate and a successful professional, climbing the ladder, working hand in hand with the people who were helping to rebuild our country. We were in two different worlds.

This bothered my husband. He became obsessed with what I might have done while he was in prison that I had not written about in my diary. He wondered how, if I really loved him, I was able to graduate from university and succeed in my career. A girl who really loved him would have fallen apart and died of a broken heart. He did not understand that I did not let myself fall apart, that I had been working myself to exhaustion to save him, to save us, to save our future. Or maybe he understood, but he didn't care. He just kept insisting that I must have cheated on him when he was away, and that I no longer needed him.

Maybe the second part was true. But I did not know that yet.

I gave him all the money I made at work, because, with his criminal record, he was unable to find a job. Instead, he spent his days hanging out with other people who did not have jobs, many of whom were connections he made in prison. After four years spent surrounded by criminals, he was welcomed into Tbilisi's criminal network with open arms, probably because they knew he understood business and finance. I had no idea of any of this. I thought that he was searching for a job or applying to finish business school.

Both of our families were working with the government to get him a presidential pardon for his crime. Amazingly, the president of Georgia had mercy on him, out of all the people in Georgia asking for pardons, and his record was wiped clean. He was lucky the commissions we appealed to saw him for who he had been when he went to prison, not the person who came out.

Once his record was clean and he was employable, one of my clients tried to help by hiring him as a corporate client manager. He did not last long in the job, and I don't know exactly why. I think my client may have discovered his secret drug addiction but did not want to embarrass me by telling me. I sometimes brought work home and did it on my computer because he insisted I come home early every night to make him dinner. I later learned he had stolen information about my corporate clients from my computer and sold it to their competitors.

***

While my marriage was struggling, conditions in my country were getting better. We were laying the bricks of the foundation of a market economy, and I was part of the generation that was building this new Georgia. The banks were growing, not just mine, introducing new products like credit cards and long-term financing that Georgians had never experienced before. That meant part of my job was educating my clients. When I sold a product, I also needed to explain how it worked and what the benefits were. And that was just the tip of the iceberg of my duties. I was doing credit-risk analysis, constructing full financials on my clients, writing memos, and creating summaries and presentations. Once we were able to prove a client was creditworthy, I was also in charge of negotiating the contracts, so I did wind up with a little bit of the corporate lawyer job I had envisioned for myself as a teenager.

My portfolio of clients included microfinance organizations, logistics and telecommunication services, all the hospitality industries, and the pharmaceutical industry—basically every sector of the Georgian economy except retail and construction. I was meeting all these people who, like me, were on the ground floor of building new products and systems. They demanded a lot of attention, always needing tailored products to address the changes they themselves were creating. I wound up in charge of new product development, because my clients were the people who always needed these new products.

It was almost like getting my MBA just through on-the-job training, instead of traveling to a university in the United States or Turkey. I saw our clients as partners in the overall project of building Georgia's economy. Instead of viewing them from the perspective of "doing my job" or "meeting my KPIs so I get the biggest bonus," I focused on long-term relationships. I always put them first and acted in their best interests because my goal was to build a stable portfolio that would help me bring in a sustainable income, rather than chase a onetime bonus.

It's also my personality—I'm always honest and direct, I don't sugarcoat bad news, and I don't waste time on being diplomatic. Sometimes it helps me, other times, maybe not so much. My direct manager used to say she wished there was a button she could push to stop me, so I could learn to be more diplomatic. If one of my older male superiors dismissed me as nothing more than a cute girl with a big smile, I did not stand for it. If someone called me out for not answering a question or providing a piece of data I thought was not relevant, I would say, "I don't give a shit about that. It doesn't make any difference in the decision-making process. Why should I have to answer this question?" I also did not like to take no for an answer. If I saw that something would work, I would do just about anything to make it happen.

I had two direct managers who were both great mentors to me. They saw the potential I had, and they also understood what my life was like outside of work and what I was going through with my husband. They wanted me to succeed and be able to earn a higher income to make up for my husband's failures and did everything they could to help me in my career. None of us work for the Bank of Georgia anymore, but I have strong relationships with both of them today.

I think the primary reason for my success was, maybe in part because of my inability to be diplomatic, I built trust with my clients. Trust is foundational to any business relationship, but it means everything in a developing country like Georgia. You want to trust that the bricks you are laying are strong enough to survive a blitz, but there are so many people, like my husband, who take shortcuts or operate without following any rules. Helping to create those rules and systems was the whole reason I studied business in the first place, and my attitude earned me the trust of people who felt the same way, who saw the importance of the work we were doing building our economy. I knew that if I ever decided to quit my job in the bank, I would be more than welcome to join any of their operations in a top-level position. I felt it everywhere. I was a part of this world.

That's what my husband was trying so hard to destroy.

***

By this time, the man I married was a full-fledged drug addict. He had moved from just yelling at me to physically abusing me—it got so bad, I came home from work one day to the announcement that his mother was throwing us out, effective immediately. She refused to tolerate our fighting any longer. We had nowhere to go, so we slept in the car that night, and the next day, I was able to find a small apartment to rent. We moved in, and my husband was free to abuse me and yell at me as much as he wanted.

After my husband wrecked my car, I knew I had to do something, so I stopped giving him money for drugs. This would send him into a rage, screaming at me and sometimes beating me. So sometimes, I would give in, just to avoid the conflict. One day when I dared to say no, he put a gun to my head and pulled the trigger. I was lucky: the bullet grazed my face and left a scratch between my ear and my eye. But then he beat me until I lost consciousness.

When I woke up, the first thing I saw was his mother's face. He had called her for help, not knowing what to do. He claimed he had no memory of hurting me, that he must have blacked out, that it was the drugs, that he had no idea what he was doing. His mother made me promise not to tell anyone. If the authorities knew her son had almost beaten me to death, they would put him back in jail. Instead, he went to a monastery for drug treatment, and I moved back into his mother's home, where I was treated by doctors who agreed to keep what they saw secret. I told my supervisors at work that I had been injured in a bad car accident and couldn't come in.

My injuries were severe—I was at risk of losing my sight in my right eye, but the doctors kept coming to treat me, and thank God I recovered without any loss. I was away from work for a month, although I started working from home much sooner than that. When I was able to stand on my feet again, I started going back to the office, although I only lasted a few hours a day for a time. Luckily, everyone believed the story that the cuts and bruises on my face came from a car accident and not the man I married.

Then my husband came back home from rehab and said that he was sorry, and that he was a changed man, and that he would never, ever use drugs or hurt me again. And we went back to living in his mother's apartment, as if nothing happened.

That's when I got pregnant.

Chapter 8

NEW DREAMS

Having a baby was literally the last thing on earth I wanted. I had stopped taking birth control pills because I had been having health problems, and the hormones exacerbated them. I was planning to switch to an IUD; I just asked my husband to use protection while I was waiting. Whenever I told him to use a condom, he accused me of not wanting his baby, because maybe I didn't really love him. It became just another thing that we fought about. Until ... surprise! I was pregnant. I did not believe this at the time, but now I'm pretty sure he did not use protection deliberately, so I would get pregnant, and he could keep me trapped.

I called my mother crying. I wasn't ready to have a baby. I was thinking of ending the pregnancy. But my mother told me that if God had given me the opportunity to have a baby, I should have the baby, and that she would be with me and stand by me every step of the way. Her words meant everything to me. Feeling her pure love, with no strings attached, when no one ever showed me love like that, helped me find my strength. I woke up the next day and made my baby the focus of everything I did, concentrating on my health, which meant trying not to get nervous and overthink things, or provoke fights with my husband.

I did everything I could do to save money, walking everywhere instead of taking the bus, checking the internet for discounts on the baby clothes and things I would need. Even four months in advance, I started stockpiling all the things I would need later because I knew that I would be overwhelmed if I tried to do it all at once.

My husband was excited about my pregnancy too—he was so happy, I hoped it was the thing that would change him, that would make him want to stay away from drugs and crime and live a good life. But it was not that thing. Soon, he was back in the cycle of using drugs, demanding money from me, and abusing me when I refused. I was afraid of what would happen to the baby if he hit me.

My health problems were also getting worse. I would lose and gain weight quickly, with no change in my eating or exercise habits. My hands shook, and I had trouble focusing my eyes. My heart rate was unstable, and sometimes I felt like I could not breathe. I assumed the constant stress of living with my husband was causing my symptoms, and I worried that also was not good for the baby, so I moved back in with my mother and grandmother. My mother evaluated my symptoms and determined that my constant stress had caused me to develop an autoimmune disease that I still suffer with today.

Moving to my mother's house did not even provide a real escape. My husband could not stand the idea of my living there and continued to pressure and threaten me. I worried what he might do if he went really crazy again. Would he kill me or kill my baby, or someone in my family? I no longer trusted my husband, and I could not control him, so the only thing I thought I could do was go back to living with him. If I gave him the money he wanted for drugs and stayed out of his way to keep myself and the baby safe, I would be OK. So I moved back into my mother-in-law's apartment.

I was in my eighth or ninth month when the police showed up at the door. They demanded to see my husband, but he escaped out the window (on the twelfth floor!) and through a neighbor's apartment. I stood there watching in disbelief as the officers tore our home apart from top to bottom. It was like being in a movie or TV show—and I was terrified. I felt like I might go into labor and have the baby right there in the apartment.

My husband went back into hiding, I continued sending money, until the police eventually caught up to him, and he was thrown back in jail for the crime of possession of drugs. I moved back to my parents' house for the rest of my pregnancy. Soon afterward, I gave birth to my daughter, Sandra. And she was, and is, beautiful.

***

Being a new mother was incredible but also difficult. I had to support my husband in jail, I had to support my baby, and the expenditures were huge. Also, I was not in good health. I was already run down from my illness and all the stress, and I got an infection in my breast from breastfeeding. Since I could not afford to buy formula, I tried my best to keep breastfeeding her, despite the pain. I was still working for the Bank of Georgia. I had been afraid to go on maternity leave because I was worried my job would not be there when I got back. So I did a lot of work from bed, with a forty-degree fever, in between caring for my newborn. I also negotiated with the prosecutors who were holding my husband to shorten his sentence. But at least I was at home with my mother, my father, my brother, and my grandmother. It was nice to be surrounded by people who loved and supported me at a time when I really needed it.

Four months after Sandra was born, I was able to make a deal with the prosecutors and, after paying yet another fee, negotiated my husband's release from jail. I made all the arrangements and moved back to his mother's house with my baby. I'll never forget the moment the car pulled up, and a few moments later, my husband walked in and saw his baby girl for the first time. He was so overcome with emotion, he could not even hold her in his hands. He looked at her and said that he had never, ever seen anything more beautiful than she was.

I burst into tears.

He was so happy, and I was happy too. I thought we had finally managed to overcome all our problems. Alexsandra represented not only hope for me, but also the hope and incentive for my husband to be a good man.

At least that's what I was hoping for.

But underneath it all, he was still a drug addict. He was still psychologically unstable. One day everything would be fine, and the next, he would make my life hell. Soon we were back in our old pattern of fighting and abuse.

I had to hire a nanny to watch Sandra. I secretly helped my mother-in-law get a job with one of my clients, although I never told her I intervened on her behalf in order to protect her pride. Her schedule would have allowed her to look after Alexsandra, but sometimes she refused to stay with her because "she had her plans." My husband watched her sometimes, but he was rarely home and not reliable, so my only option to keep my baby safe and do my job was to hire someone to look after her. Every month, I withdrew a secret amount of cash from my salary and hid it, so I would be able to pay the nanny—otherwise, my husband might take the money. Sometimes he did, and I had to apologize to the nanny and tell her she would need to wait to be paid. As it was, between the loans for all my husband's legal problems and our living expenses, there was never enough money for all the things I needed to pay for. I was a college graduate with an important job at a bank, and sometimes I could not join my friends for lunch because I couldn't pay. It was embarrassing and humiliating.

My coworkers were more than willing to foot the bill for me—they were like my family. Everyone at the bank knew about my situation with my husband, and everyone was kind and supportive, especially my department head, whom I still call Wonder Woman. They all looked out for me and even collected money around the office to help me. But it was never enough to make a real difference in my circumstances. I was married to a drug addict and criminal who held me like a prisoner. I could not escape.

Several times, I took my daughter back to my parents' house and asked my husband for a divorce, but every time, he refused to consent. Instead, he would harass and threaten me, so I worried what he might do to my family or my daughter. As hard as it was to live with him, he made life harder when I was away. Then we would reach a point where he would say he was sorry and promise to change, and blame all his bad behavior on his bad luck in getting arrested and the drugs, and say how much he loved me. I would decide to give him another chance, and move back in, and stay until it got so bad I had to leave again. It was an endless cycle.

Then, miraculously, during one of our separations, he consented to a divorce. I legally ended the marriage and looked forward to rebuilding my life. But it did not make any difference. Soon he was chasing me again, threatening me, saying he would call my employers and tell lies that would destroy my reputation at work. Once he ambushed me on my way home from work and grabbed my phone and ran off with it so he could see who I had been talking to. One day my babysitter called me in a panic, because my now-ex-husband was following her, asking where Sandra was, acting like he was going to do something terrible.

It was like living in a nightmare. I reached a point where I could not function. I wasn't able to focus on my work; I felt like I couldn't protect my daughter. And then he changed again. He told me that he loved me, that he was ready to start everything over, that he wanted to be a father to his daughter. So even though we were divorced, I moved back in with him one more time. It was my self-defense tactic—and while it was not a good one, it was the only thing I thought I could do to control my circumstances.

I started to fantasize about an escape, about taking my child somewhere far away, where he could not get to me. At the time, I'd initially received an attractive, well-paid job offer from my client to become their CFO. I'd shared it with bank management, who asked me to stay on a few additional months to see through the work managing seven sectors and to help with that transition. I worked so hard during that time, feeling responsible to the bank where I'd learned so much.

But suddenly another blitz began. There was another revolution in my country, and the governing party changed. Many companies started to be investigated, and one of them was the company where I was going. The investigations usually translated into assets being frozen until the matter of the investigation was resolved. In rare cases like ours, they'd even take materials like computers and other hardware from the companies.

Because of this circumstance, the bank refused to provide money to this company to continue the project, and I could do nothing about it. Unfortunately, the relationship between the two organizations got very tense, and actions were taken against both the bank and me.

This did not sit well with me, so I ended up refusing the job offer. Interestingly, not long before this turmoil began, the man who would later become my boyfriend and the father to my son was hired as a financial analyst in that company. Later, with his help, the company overcame that hardship. He has since become the CFO. So karma put everything right.

Given those changes and the pressures that came along with them, I began preparing documents to apply to study abroad. I applied to different scholarship and grant programs designed to facilitate educational opportunities for single mothers, because I was drowning in loans and had no chance to get additional finances from anywhere. Still, after everything I had been through, could moving to another country with a baby and getting my MBA with no help from anyone be any harder than what I had already survived? I still had my dreams, and I desperately wanted something else out of life. I wanted to leave the bank and get my MBA and take my baby with me. I thought I could escape by running away from my problems—I did not realize that distance would not actually make those problems go away.

A good friend helped me come to my senses—and let me know he knew of a different kind of opportunity that would keep me closer to home. A company was looking for a deputy CFO; they were growing rapidly but also experiencing some financial difficulties and thought bringing in "new blood" would help them implement innovative solutions. My friend recommended me. I told him I was not interested, but he convinced me to at least go see what these people were proposing. Then I could decide what I wanted to do with the rest of my life.

I went to interview with the CFO who needed a deputy, as well as the current CEO of the holding company that had this growing company I interviewed with in its holdings. I walked into the interview dressed in a green jacket, ripped jeans, red ballet shoes, and French braids. I did not look like a financial genius or like someone trying to land a high-powered job. I looked more like a schoolgirl. But the

CEO I met with appreciated the fact that I was 100 percent myself. He trusted me, and I liked and trusted him too. We had a great conversation about his vision and what he was trying to bring to Georgia.

The CEO told me I was wasting my talent on one company and offered me a bigger horizon, a horizon of being the CFO of a holding company, where I would be responsible not only for the company under discussion but also the entire assets held by the shareholder. These assets spanned many different sectors in Georgia's emerging economy, and the CEO was looking for an organized structure to manage them all and help him put things in order and do them the right way, with transparency and integrity and according to the rules of the global economy.

It was a very exciting opportunity. Still, joining this company, which was called CBS Group, would be a leap of faith. First because, at this point, there was not really a company to speak of at all. There were neither employees nor any specific assets—just scattered shares owned by a particular founder with a mission to do something big and transformational. My job would be to work with him to assemble all of it, refine it, and nurture its growth. And since this CEO believed I had too much talent to be a deputy CFO, he told me that if I joined the company, I would be its CFO.

This challenge resonated deeply with me. I loved helping my clients build things, and now I would be on that side of the process, in such a high position, where my decisions would have real impact. But I would be leaving a stable job with a consistent salary, which was crucial for me financially. And I would be giving up my chance to escape my husband.

Could I really risk it for this chance to build something independently?

In the end, I decided to go for it.

Chapter 9

THE BREAKING POINT

When I started at CBS Group in 2013, I had one job: to clean things up.

The companies in our holdings were a lot like the overall business environment in Georgia at the time. There was an ocean between them and the rest of the developed world when it came to things like compliance, good governance, or adherence to any kind of standard. Some regulations had been put in place nationally, and some people were eager to embrace them, but for every company that welcomed the changes that would be necessary if we were to join the global economy, there were a lot more that preferred doing things the old way. Why should they report their earnings and pay taxes to the government when they could make more money off the books, on the black market, through secret deals or bribery, or from just plain stealing?

CBS Group was one of the companies that wanted to make change. The four of us—our shareholder, my CEO, our office manager, and I—were all on the same mission: to place our company at the forefront of this new, transparent way of doing business in Georgia. If we were going to grow our assets, acquire additional holdings, and develop into the kind of company we dreamed we could create, we needed to start with a strong foundation. I went in there with my brush and my broom, ready to clean things up.

And oh my God, they were a mess. Our shareholder wasn't even sure of exactly what he had in terms of assets. He had no idea what the companies in his holdings were worth or what his liabilities were. The only way to know was to clean up and structure all the assets to see a clear picture of what was there. Once we had that, we could decide what to do with each asset according to our strategies for development and risk diversification. My plan was to sell some holdings for the cash we needed to fund the operation; develop the rest into strong, legitimate, taxpaying businesses; and eventually, acquire additional assets that fit in with our overall strategy. Everything was done with the goal of increasing value for the shareholder while also increasing the value of the companies. That way, the shareholder would continue to see a stable income while I rebuilt his assets according to international standards.

Before any of that could happen, I needed to know everything that was going on in these companies. I had to go into each individual business and look at their operations and their books to get a clear picture of what they were doing, right and wrong, legal and illegal, so I could build on their strengths and try to fix whatever problems existed. But not everyone involved was on board with this plan.

Both middle and top managers at some of these companies went to great lengths to stop me from learning what they were up to. They put obstacles in my way, refusing to share the information I requested and, more importantly, hiding where the company's money was coming from and where it was going. Since I needed this information to do my job properly, I became a financial detective, digging into the companies' records on my own to see what was working properly and what was not.

I had to start from scratch, and I had to be creative. For example, one of the holdings was a chain of restaurants, and the only way for me to know how much money was going in and out was to stand in front of the place and physically count the people coming in, look over every single check, and compare them to determine the amount of the average bill. Then I compared those numbers against their procurement costs and counted the inventory and raw material as well; I dug into the recipes and calculated the waste and residuals, at which point I was finally able to see how much of what was going in the accounting system was legitimate and how much was dark money.

I approached each of the holding company's different businesses the same way, digging deep into all the contracts and evaluating each and every transaction, as well as the market prices of the services and products we were purchasing and selling. I found lots of shady things that were being done by lots of people, so I did what I needed to do to stop them.

Suddenly—and not surprisingly—I had haters.

Now instead of my ex-husband, I had a bunch of corporate managers chasing me all over Tbilisi, sneaking a device on my computer to record my private messages, spying on me, and trying a range of different tactics to convince me to stop what I was doing. They tried being nice, reminding me of how hard my life was, offering to repay the massive pile of loans I had been forced to take out to support my husband and try to get him out of prison. When bribery didn't work, they tried threatening me, saying if I did not stop digging into their books, they were going to get me fired from my job. When I still didn't stop, they showed our shareholder proof of my ex-husband's criminal convictions. They tried to convince my shareholder that I was involved in the scheme, that my ex and I were partners in crime, that I could not be trusted. But my shareholder knew me better than that. My CEO knew me better than that. They trusted me, and I did not lose my job.

This was all unfolding during one of those rare periods when my ex-husband was also working. I had used my connections when he was just out of prison to help him get a corporate client manager position with one of my client companies, and that provided him the job experience needed to be hired as an IT and systems integrator at a telco equipment and software provider. After he was released from prison the second time, he'd secured a C-level position with an Armenian firm (with access to the company accounts, which turned out to be a terrible mistake). He paid me back for my help by insisting that, since he was working, I should not be working at all.

One day when I came back from work, he was in hysterics about an alleged affair, screaming, even taking a hammer from the wardrobe and hitting me in the knee. I still have problems with that knee—yet another reminder: when you are being abused, don't let it bring you to your knees. Use them for running away instead. But by this point, this sort of abuse was all expected behavior from my ex-husband, and I had grown used to it. What I did not expect were the other ways he threatened my career.

The Armenian company where my ex-husband worked was a supplier of telecommunications equipment for the most important company in our holdings—the first company that laid cable under the Black Sea, connecting Georgia to Europe (specifically Bulgaria) via the internet. The Armenian company had entered into a tender offer announced by the holding company.

As you might imagine, it was a very, very strategically important asset. At the same time, it was one of the companies most in need of cleaning up. It had a huge bank loan, and the structure of the company was very complicated. Plus, the management team was not necessarily up to the task of protecting the company's value or stopping shady and illegal things from happening. The bank was about to default the company and sell the assets. My initiative was to clean up this company and sell it ourselves because otherwise, the shareholders would have lost everything. The best strategy was to sell the same company twice by dividing it into independent running units: the retail and the wholesale business. That period involved a restructuring of the company—heavy due diligence processes and preparations for bids. I traveled extensively for these negotiations with potential buyers because it involved international interested parties as well. This period was so heavy in many different ways: my haters, my personal life, my career, my health. Once they realized my ex-husband worked for this telecommunications company's suppliers, they saw their opening. Given their mistrust and misunderstanding of my initiative, my haters had accused me of sharing confidential information with my husband and fraudulently enabling him to win the bid and get the cash back on the transaction. They wanted to stop me from digging deep and changing the management to fulfill the strategy described above.

Meanwhile, he was continuing to create chaos with whomever he encountered. Once, when I received an encouraging email from an ex-colleague from the bank, a former legal administrator in my sector, my ex found and read the message. My ex called him, made threats, and asked to meet up. When they did, my ex intentionally hit him with a car that belonged to the Armenian company. Not only were my colleague and his friend seriously injured, but three nearby cars were also damaged.

Unbelievably, these incidents were used as ammunition to claim I was dishonest and thus I must have had this relationship with the legal administrator. But my former colleague had come to my defense, printing every last email between us, showing nothing untoward had happened.

When police came to take testimony, out of respect for me, he and his friend withdrew their claims, and no case against my ex was opened. I have never been able to find this person again, to say thank you and to apologize about everything that happened.

To make matters worse, my ex had, in fact, been stealing from the Armenian company that supplied the company in our holdings for almost as long as he had been working there. He'd even bought a car, saying that it was my birthday gift. Though he did not have a driver's license, he and his brother drove it more than I did. When his brother got into an accident, he'd totaled the car and damaged both a school fence and a billboard! Another loss. I wrote it off, sold it in parts, and paid for the damages. And how was that car financed? It was bought with stolen money from the company. And I had absolutely no idea.

When my ex got caught, all hell broke loose for me. My haters insisted there was no way I was not involved, and that CBS Group needed to get rid of me. Again, because my shareholder knew me and believed in me, I did not lose my job—my initiatives were working. We actually did change the CEO and made some structural changes in the management as well, negotiated the terms with the bank, and—step-by-step—implemented the strategy. One of the main reasons the bank even opened for the negotiations was a result of the steps taken by CBS.

The CFO, who also happened to be one of the best telecommunications specialists in the industry, defended (and befriended) me. But the Armenian company still wanted justice: their accusation was that he had exceeded his official duties and embezzled a large amount from the company's assets. They wanted to make him cover the amount taken out of the company; if not, they were threatening to put him in prison.

Once again, it was up to me to save my ex-husband from himself. No matter what he had done to me, he loved our daughter, and she loved him, and I did not want Sandra to have the stigma of having a prisoner for a father. She had been bullied in kindergarten and later at school for having a criminal for a father. I saw how this hurt her. Because I had never told her the true story of why her father was always away, she also felt a grievance against me for not telling the truth. So I knew I had to do something to stop him from being sent to jail for nine years. I started negotiations with the company, and I even visited the founders in Armenia. I asked them to arrange partial payments, and I would pay that amount. But the Armenians refused, saying that he committed the crime and that he should pay for it. They'd put a lot of trust in him, which he betrayed. In this period of negotiations, I had an ally named Natia who stood by me like a wall, helping me with every difficulty I faced. It was excruciatingly difficult.

During this time I'd been in negotiations with the Armenians, the police hadn't yet begun searching for my ex. The Armenians' intentions at that time were expressly to keep him out of jail, because they knew that, in the event he landed in jail, they would never receive any money.

But my ex had a US visa. He had a host family. So he'd asked me to finance his trip to the United States, where he would find work and cover his losses. And I did finance that. I financed it all because it gave me precious space to breathe. I needed a moment to think about the blitz bursting over my head. But as it turned out, he only ended up being there for several months. Being an addict, he was unable to find a job. I could not (and would not) cover the additional costs he needed to survive there. He returned to Georgia, and soon afterward, the police had him in their sights.

At this point, I had not told Sandra the truth about her father. When he was away in jail or off doing God-knows-what, I would tell her that he was off working for us. When you're a kid, you don't really understand things like why your father does not live with you, or why your father hates your mother, so I tried to protect my child from these kinds of painful truths. But it wasn't just about my daughter. I really did want my former husband to be free and happy. When he was free and happy, everything was easier for all of us. Plus, there was always the hope that some miracle would happen and he would come to his senses and decide to turn his life around and get better.

I think, in a way, I always felt responsible for my ex-husband's problems. My first impression was of a boy so in love with me it made him crazy, so crazy he flunked out of university. So that was who my brain decided he was: a tragic hero in a romantic drama. Every time he did a crazy thing, whether it was lighting candles under my window or accusing me of having affairs with coworkers, I'd attributed it all to his love for me and to the things that happened, like the drugs and the brain damage, when he was in jail for killing the gangster to save his friend. Of course, his problems were not his fault! I continued to view him as a tragic person who was desperately in love with me. I was so wrapped up in this narrative that I missed about a million red flags indicating something very different was going on.

I remember one day, I'd gotten a phone call from a woman in Sweden looking for her daughter. She thought the phone she was calling belonged to my then-husband, and she thought her daughter was with him. When I told her I was the wife of the man whose number she thought she was calling, the call suddenly dropped. But I didn't give it any thought.

Another time, I accidentally came across nude photos of a girl along with love letters to my husband. I told him what I saw, and he told me she was just some crazy girl who was in love with him, that it meant nothing to him. I believed him.

Sometimes he would run out of gigabytes on his phone and would use mine to go on Facebook or send messages. Afterward, he would forget to log out, and I would sometimes scroll past conversations between him and different women. When I asked him what was going on, he always had an explanation. I believed them all.

But during his escape to Turkey, I had his phones, and I had space to breathe and think. I was finally able to put the pieces together. And it became obvious pretty quickly that I had been living a lie. After I found pictures of him having fun with the girl in Sweden whose mother had called me, as well as a child's baptism photo, my ex admitted he and this girl had a son. Soon afterward, I learned that he'd even brought Sandra to get to know her brother when they'd visited Georgia.

From there, I quickly started to piece things together. When he'd gone to Sweden the first time, he was working for a client company where I'd gotten him a job. He was there as a corporate client manager, but no money had been wired for the travel. And I remembered then what he and his mother had been hiding from me. When he traveled to Sweden, they hid the traditional Georgian food to be taken to Sweden for them in a neighbor's apartment. He took these from the neighbor just before he left for the airport. Clearly, this relationship had been going on in parallel for several years.

Eventually, before his escape to Turkey, she'd even visited him in Batumi—in the home that I rented and paid for! He had been lying to both of us for many years, telling her we were divorced and sending photos of me packing my things. She'd later come to my office to apologize, to talk with me. I really felt every pain that girl had to go through. I wished her luck; we agreed that we were happy for each other to both finally be free of all that mess. And even now, I have her on my Facebook, and we always wish each other happy birthday.

Back in that moment when she came to see me, I knew my husband had given me a divorce not because he wanted to do the right thing—he did it so he could send proof to this poor girl that he was free and available! The girl and I had a good talk. She had learned a lesson as well.

More and more emails and messages—it was revealed that he had been cheating on me with multiple women, for years and years. Of course, I had seen some of this evidence before, but I had always chosen not to believe it. I could not believe it because I never stopped seeing my ex-husband as a man driven crazy by his love for me. In that moment, I realized that "love" had been a lie. And whatever love I had left for him died at that moment.

Once he'd admitted to the baby, I left. And the next morning when I arrived at work, I got on the internet and started looking for an apartment. Within three hours, I found the perfect place for Sandra and me—it was highly undervalued because the owner was experiencing financial difficulties and needed someone to take the place off his hands. I really wanted the apartment, but I needed to make a deposit right away, before someone else beat me to it. And I had no money. In that moment when I needed an out, I'd told a few friends about it. I had asked if they could help. And somehow, within an hour, a huge group of people, including my former colleagues at the bank, had all come together to fund my own escape. They were like my angels. I had all the money I needed to secure the apartment in my hand. I left my mother-in-law's apartment and moved into our new home with my daughter in one night.

Unbelievably, he came to our home, pleading for help. He cried that he would not be able to withstand prison anymore and that it was better for him to kill himself. He cut himself with a knife right in front of me, giving a real impression that he would kill himself. As he had done several times before, he simulated hanging himself. I was really very scared, so I continued to do my best to send him where he wanted. I thought that would also help me find the slightest serenity for a while, that in that way, everything might settle down.

So that's how I found myself taking out another huge loan to send my abusive, criminal, now-proven cheater of an ex-husband to Turkey—just one of the expenses I incurred in my endless quest to keep him alive and out of jail.

Once he was safe there, I even took Sandra and his mother to Turkey to visit him, as his mother was worried, and Sandra wanted to see whether her father was really "working" there.

***

Then about a year and a half after I moved out, I got a phone call in the middle of the night. It was my mother-in-law's neighbor, who also lived on the twelfth floor, in the apartment where my husband had climbed in through the window and escaped when I was pregnant with Sandra. She told me I needed to come right away, that something terrible had happened to my brother-in-law. I had always supported my brother-in-law, even helping him to finance his studies in Belarus. Yes, I would do whatever I could to help him, of course. So when I learned the call was about him, and that my mother-in-law needed my help, I responded right away.

I called my mother to stay with Sandra and hurried over to the apartment. The moment I arrived, I knew what had happened. I saw the emergency vehicles and personnel clustered around an area directly below my mother-in-law's apartment. I looked up to the window and saw a smaller group of officials, looking around, taking notes, doing "official-looking" things.

The elevator wasn't working—probably because the emergency personnel were using it—so I climbed the stairs to the twelfth floor and found the neighbor, who explained what had happened. She heard a loud argument between my mother-in-law and her son, and then my mother-in-law started screaming. Right after that, my mother-in-law called the neighbor and asked her to look through the window and tell her what she saw. She had locked herself in a room and couldn't bring herself to do it.

Like his father before him, my brother-in-law had attempted suicide. The neighbor saw that my brother-in-law had jumped from the window of the twelfth-floor apartment where I used to live. She told my mother-in-law the truth: that my brother-in-law was still alive but in grave condition. He was rushed to the hospital and into surgery, but he did not survive.

By that time, another relative had come to the apartment to break the news, and together, we went to my former mother-in-law and told her that her son was dead. It was one of the hardest, most heartbreaking things I've ever had to do.

It was even harder because her other son, my ex-husband, was still in Turkey, and he was unable to come back. Not only was he still on the run from the law in Georgia, but he was also now in hiding from the police in Turkey. He had been arrested for drugs, and while they were taking him to jail, he escaped by asking to use the toilet and jumping out a third-story window. He broke both legs but still managed to get away. There was no threat of his being found—once you go into hiding in Turkey, the government will not spend resources to find you. Still, there was no possibility of his coming home, so I was the one who helped my mother-in-law organize his brother's funeral services and burial. Then I went with her to Turkey so she could break the news to my ex-husband in person.

When we found my ex-husband, he was so strung out on drugs, he couldn't even grasp what his mother was saying. He could not even understand that his brother was dead. He was a lost cause.

My brother-in-law and I had been very close—he was just a boy when I'd moved in, so we had almost grown up together. He shared things with me he never shared with his mother or his brother and had grown into a young, beautiful man with his whole life ahead of him. And now, like his father before him, he had taken his own life.

I visited his grave very often; he had so often protected me from his brother. But when my ex was released from jail, he wrote to say that he would kill me if I visited the grave again. So I stopped. After he was put in prison again (and even now), I started to visit his brother's grave again. I do not bring flowers anymore, and to avoid being noticed, I go only during times when I am sure nobody will be there.

His passing was so incredibly, crushingly sad. And my heart broke for my mother-in-law, who was such a tragic person. Not only had she lost her husband and her youngest son to suicide, but her oldest was also killing himself with drugs. In that moment, I didn't care about the ways my mother-in-law had hurt me; as a mother myself, I was able to support another woman in this way. I only wanted to take away some of her pain. I wanted to do the human thing.

So I decided I would get my ex-husband out of Turkey. Maybe I would be able to save one son for my mother-in-law.

***

Once again, I threw myself into the project of rescuing my ex-husband. This was a big challenge because he was still in a lot of trouble in Georgia. He was still facing nine years in prison for his crimes against the Armenians, but now there were additional charges because he had also crossed the border into Turkey illegally, through the Adzharian mountains; Ajara is an autonomous region of Georgia that borders Turkey. There was no way he could come back to Georgia without a plea bargain with the regional government; otherwise, he would have been thrown in jail by the prosecutor's office immediately for many years. So I worked with the prosecutors and officials across both regions and got them to agree to a pardon and a reduced sentence. Then I advised my ex to return legally, and he did. He was arrested at the border and taken to jail. He was sentenced to one year for the border crossing and was sent out of Ajara, where he was given a higher sentence, which was the prevailing one. With the plea bargain, he was jailed for fewer than two years all told and able to escape the repayment of the funds. Once again, I paid whatever fines were required to make this happen.

Following our trip to Turkey, his mother was so disappointed in her son that despite all my hard work getting him home, she wanted nothing to do with him. She refused to visit him in jail or send him money or food, so since it had been my idea to get him out of Turkey in the first place, that all fell to me. I sent him clothes, money, and food, and even visited him in jail. Maybe I didn't need to do all those things, following rules I made up for myself. Maybe I was being stupid, assuming responsibility for him yet again. But I could not help feeling a human connection to this man, wanting to help him, wanting him to finally get better and live up to the promise he had shown so many years before. I guess I'm just not a very vengeful person. When people hurt me, I don't wish pain upon them in return.

Plus, he was still my daughter's father. I wanted her to have a father who was not a criminal, not a drug abuser, not a failure.

I was so worried the situation with her father would diminish her life in some way that Sandra became the focus of my life. I was determined that she would never, ever suffer, and that meant giving her everything I had that wasn't already going to her father. I sent her to the best kindergarten in town, and after that, the best primary school. When she had vacations, I financed trips for her and my mother to travel all over Georgia together. My mother played a big role in Sandra's development, nurturing her, developing her interest in music and the arts, and teaching her about social responsibility, as did my Russian grandmother. I was too worried to see it then, but today I realize, from an early age, my daughter grew up surrounded by strong women who loved her. And that made her strong.

There are actually a lot of parallels between the way I raised Sandra and the way I was raised, by parents and grandparents who tried to give me everything, even when times were hard. There was just one giant, glaring difference. I had a father who loved his family and always stood by us, no matter what. My daughter's father was a criminal who, it was clear, cared only about himself. There was nothing I could do that could ever make up for that. It was like my original sin of letting myself fall in love with my ex-husband, when something deep inside always told me it would end badly, was going to haunt me forever.

This really was the first time I tried to quantify all the damage my ex had caused over the years. I thought about the ways he endangered his daughter's happiness, how he destroyed my dreams, and how he brought stress and shame to my mother and father, and even my grandparents. And what had he given us in return? Nothing but cheating and lies and abuse. This could not possibly be love. When you love someone, you care about their happiness and well-being.

From the very beginning, my ex had never cared really about mine, let alone his daughter's. Even when he was showering me with presents, in reality, he always, always put himself first. I knew it had to stop. When his sentence was up, we needed new ground rules moving forward.

I wrote him a letter in prison, telling him that after taking some time to think things through, I realized I could not love a person who cheated on me and treated me the way he did and that our relationship was over. I told him I would help him get out of jail and continue to support him and his mother, but that my support should not be mistaken for love or for any desire to live together again. The support I was giving him was really for our daughter, so that she would not grow up with a criminal father who lived in poverty and shame. I wrote that I was giving him one last opportunity, and I hoped he would not take it for granted. I hoped that when he got out of jail this time, he would finally behave himself and try to be a good person for his daughter.

But the next time I visited him in jail, and we talked about the letter, it was like he never even read it. He had no interest in what I was asking him for; he wanted to keep the drama going. He accused me of having another lover, of leaving him because I no longer loved him, of being the real cheater in our relationship.

But this time, I was over it. I told him my only mission was to get him out of jail, and after that, I didn't want to know anything about him. I hoped he would be a good father to my daughter, but if he was not, I was going to do everything in my power to stop the relationship.

A few months later, when he was released from jail, he sent me a message:

"I'm out, and now I'm going to make your life hell."

Chapter 10

THIS IS WAR

One morning not long after my husband got out of jail, I woke up to a very unpleasant surprise. The whole internet was full of nude pictures of me.

Apparently, at some point in our relationship, my ex had secretly taken photos of me coming out of the shower. He had saved these photos for years, I guess waiting for just the right moment to pull them out to use them against me. And he had found that moment. He created an entire website dedicated to me, with the naked pictures, details like my height and weight, and a list of the nasty things I liked to do with men—because the "purpose" of the website was to advertise my "services" as a prostitute. It had to have taken him days to put it all together—there were links to YouTube videos of women engaged in various sexual activities that he presented as me, although they were not. He sent links to every single person on my contact list—my friends, my bosses, even my clients. And of course, since the site was supposed to be advertising a "business," he helpfully included my phone number. My phone rang day and night—there were hundreds of phone calls from men seeking my services.

He had finally done what he always threatened to do. He destroyed my dignity in front of everyone I knew.

***

The warning I'd received was true. My ex was devoting his postprison life to a one-man mission to destroy me. He kept up the false narrative of how I'd found another lover and abandoned him while he was stuck in jail and unable to stop me. His mother forgot about how angry she had been when he failed to recognize his brother was dead and came back around to his side. He was her only surviving child, so I guess it made sense that even though she had known me for years, even though I had done nothing but try to help her and save her son, she chose to believe every horrible thing he said about me. When I took Sandra to see her grandmother, she would repeat those things word for word, saying I was not a good mother, and that I left her father because I was a cheater. But I kept taking her granddaughter to see her. It was my duty. I was used to that sort of abuse when it came to my ex.

But this time, the harassment was scarier than ever before. He followed me everywhere, threatening me. One night I was coming home from work late when he jumped out of the darkness, put a knife to my throat, and demanded money. Another time, I was working on one of the biggest mergers in the history of my country, and he revealed that, when we still lived together, he had stolen passwords and accessed confidential data about the merger (and even had information he'd stolen previously as well) from my computer about one of the companies involved, and threatened to make the information public. Another time, he took Sandra out for a "walk," then sent me a message saying I would never see my daughter again if I didn't give him money. I went to the police after that because he had essentially kidnapped my daughter, but since he was also Sandra's father, the police did not take me seriously. Women in Georgia had very limited rights against their husbands, including ex-husbands, so he was free to continue his mission of making my life hell.

Once the porn site was launched, I had to change my phone number, but it was complicated. My number was also the contact number for all my clients; it was basically my whole professional identity, and now it had been compromised. While I worked on untangling all of that, I asked a very IT-savvy friend to follow the IP address and figure out where the website came from. I reported the porn site, and the YouTube videos, and all the social networks, and all my friends and clients who received the links also reported them. After about a month, everything was cleared. But the damage had been done. Everyone I knew had seen me naked, even my clients. I was afraid to show my face on the street.

By this point, I could no longer hide the truth about my ex from my family. My father had started acting as my bodyguard, following me home at night to protect me from surprise encounters with my ex. My father also asked a relative to go and warn him that if he would not stop, we were going to sue him. This was a humane action on my father's part, done just to give him a choice; I do not know whether the message was delivered, but nothing stopped. And after his imprisonment, my ex's mother claimed that she knew nothing about her son's actions. She said had she known, she would have stopped him.

My brother, Konstantine, vowed to kill him the next time he saw him. It was crazy. I had kept the worst parts of my marriage secret so my family wouldn't worry about me, and now they were ready to commit crimes and sacrifice their freedom for me. They felt like they had no other choice, because nobody with any official power would do anything. I went to the police multiple times, and they kicked me out every time, saying, "It's a family affair, and we don't care." They told me that they couldn't do anything to my ex-husband without proof of the things he was doing to me.

Proof. I had found proof before, when I started at CBS Group and had to investigate all our holdings. I could certainly do that again.

My CEO and shareholders at CBS Group put me in touch with the right people in the government who could help me, and I went about finding and compiling all the proof I could of my ex-husband's crimes against me. Every evening after work, I would go to the police department and work on writing the case—all those lessons my grandfather taught me about the law were finally being put to good use. I just never imagined I would be using them to protect myself from the man I'd married.

The police made it clear that just telling my story, bad as it was, would not be enough. I needed to find physical evidence of the threats, abuse, theft, and extortion my ex had committed against me. Without empirical evidence that could prove these things happened, I had no case. So I got a court order that allowed the police to listen to and record my phone, so they could track who was (and had been) on the other end of the line and listen to any conversations with my ex. I personally communicated with the telephone operators and with providers at Gmail, Yahoo, and Microsoft Exchange to get the hard evidence that proved my ex had stolen information from my system. I was also able to produce evidence showing he was directly responsible for the website that said I was a prostitute.

I brought all this evidence to the police, but they said it would only prove that I had been threatened. That would only put my ex in jail for a year or so, which meant he would be back out and tormenting me again soon. I needed him to go away and stay gone for as long as possible. So I kept digging.

I was able to find proof that my ex had kidnapped our daughter, but the law around a child being kidnapped by a parent was murky. What the police really wanted, what they promised would put my ex away for a long time, was proof of extortion. And they came up with a plan for me to help them get what they wanted in a very dramatic way. They asked me to participate in a sting operation, like something you'd see in a movie. I would hide a recording device on my body, under my clothes where no one could see it. I would meet my ex-husband where he suggested—in a public place if I was afraid, or at an agreed-upon apartment—or I would leave money in a designated spot. And I would make a payoff to him using bills the police had marked to ensure he couldn't claim it was his own and so that, wherever he spent that money, it could be traced. The police officers would be nearby, so they could catch him in the act of committing the crime and come to my rescue if things went sideways during the "sting."

This sounded like a very bad idea to me. I had seen a lot of movies and TV shows where a person wore a wire to catch a criminal, but this was not the movies. What if my ex discovered the recording equipment? What if he got angry? How could I trust that the police would be there in time to help if he came after me with a knife again, or even a gun? Our police didn't really answer these questions and concerns I had with the certainty I needed. I already knew he was capable of hurting me, and I was pretty sure he wouldn't think twice about killing me. He had almost done it before.

But there were other reasons beyond fear that I did not like the plan. I also did not want to have any direct involvement, besides what I had already done, in putting my ex in jail. Reporting crimes he had committed and was continuing to commit against me was one thing—that was only for my own protection. Tricking him into committing another crime, even if that meant he would be locked away in jail for a longer period of time, was not something I felt right about. When our daughter got older and asked how and why her father went to jail, I did not want to have to tell her that I participated in the sting operation that sent him there. It would be another opportunity for him to tell lies about me and hurt me more, and I saw no way it could benefit my child.

So I told the police officers that even if the evidence I had already provided was not enough, I was still not going to participate in their plan. I had three hundred pages of proof of other crimes my ex had committed against me that I had written up for them, and I trusted that somewhere in there was enough evidence to send my ex to jail. I sent everything to the prosecutor, and it turned out there was enough that they were able to catch my ex in the act of stealing money from my account. At that point, he was arrested and sent back to jail for the fifth time, to await trial.

Of course, my mother-in-law was devastated at the prospect of her only surviving son going back to jail again. When the court proceedings started, she tried to get the case thrown out over a loan we had taken out together, saying I had taken the money for myself instead of telling the truth, which was that, like most of my loans, it was obtained to either help her son survive in or get out of prison. Thank God I was paying this loan back in a timely manner and had proof that I had paid it directly to the prosecutor's office, or maybe they would have believed her. As it was, my ex's lawyers couldn't believe I had so much proof of all the things my ex had done. They tried to soften the case against him, but in addition to physical proof, I also had witnesses, all of whom spoke against my husband and on my behalf. In the end, the case was overwhelming, and the judge convicted him of both theft and extortion. She said the evidence I had provided was more than enough.

Part of the reason my case was so complicated was that it was the first case in Georgia involving extortion between family members. It was a big, groundbreaking case, and the police had been afraid of losing it, because they knew they would look like heroes if they won. That was why they wanted me to do their work for them by wearing a wire and tricking my ex into breaking the law one more time, live, while they were listening. They wanted that irrefutable, 100 percent proof, even if they had to risk my life one more time to get it and show what big, heroic policemen they were. Luckily, the evidence I worked to provide was enough for the prosecutor to prove the case to the judge and jury. My ex was sentenced to nine years in jail—three more years than his first sentence for killing that gangster in self-defense back when we were still in university.

After twelve years, the blitz on my life was over. I was finally free.

***

One day, about eight months after my ex was sent to jail, I was bringing Sandra to or from school when my former mother-in-law suddenly popped up in front of our home. She wanted something from me. She wanted me to take back the story I had told the police and the court about all the crimes her son had committed against me so they would let him out of prison. It was clear to me that she still had no idea what her son had actually done to me—or if she did, she was in denial. Of course he told his mother a different story, but it was still her choice to believe it. She had every single time before, even when he almost killed me. Why should this time be any different?

She asked me why I had done this terrible thing and taken her only son away from her and sent him to jail. I said that one day she would thank me: I had saved him from death one more time because jail would give him an opportunity to recover from his drug addiction.

I also shared that it was the only way I could protect my family and myself because the situation was aggravated, and I simply could not let my father and brother get involved in any problems because of me. I had no choice; he would not leave me alone or stop trying to destroy my life, and I had no other way of making it stop. I told her that, for that reason, I could not give her what she wanted. She looked at me and said that if I refused to get her son out of prison, she cursed me with the same fate that she had with her younger son. My former mother-in-law told me, right in front of her grandchild, that she hoped that grandchild would die.

As a mother, and as a woman, I always tried to understand her tragedy. I remembered the good days for Sandra and me with her. I'd helped her however I could, even financing their stays during the winter holidays in mountain resorts. I had been showing her all along that, regardless of my relationship with her son, I would work to keep Sandra close to her roots. She loved Sandra. Sandra loved her too. Sandra grew up with her. I could not understand how she could possibly say this. I never brought my daughter to see her grandmother again.

Not long afterward, I applied to the court to terminate my ex's parental rights toward Sandra. I wanted a complete termination, but the judge said that wouldn't be a good outcome for my daughter, because if through some miracle her father were to have any assets when he died, Sandra would not be able to inherit them if their legal connection was completely severed. So instead of a total restriction, the judge imposed a partial restriction, which is actually the perfect arrangement for our circumstance. My daughter has the right to contact her father if she wants to, but my ex has no rights whatsoever when it comes to my daughter. He can't see her or contact her or ask for anything without getting my consent first.

It was a long war, but in the end, I won.

Chapter 11

FREE AT LAST

For the first time since I was seventeen years old, I was finally free. But I couldn't exactly feel my newfound freedom. I was too worried about my daughter. After the incident with my former mother-in-law, she was afraid to be alone, afraid that her grandmother would track her down and make good on her promise to end her life. I felt like there was no way her mental health would not suffer, because of things like these and because her father was not only in prison, but also in prison for crimes he had committed against her mother. It was the opposite of the loving, stable family I grew up with.

With the help of my family and my friends, I was able to find a good, professional psychologist to talk to Sandra. I was very relieved to learn that, in his opinion, she did not need a lot of help. He told me she was positive and strong and had a healthy attitude toward life.

He said I needed more help than she did.

***

The psychologist was right. I was not in a very good place. My entire life had been one battle after another—as soon as I solved one problem, another would pop up—like a nightmare version of the carnival game Whack-A-Mole. I was a successful, young professional woman with a great career, but my finances were in shambles because I spent so much money supporting the person who caused all those problems. The one real mistake I made in my life—trusting a person I knew in my heart I should not trust—led to a blitz that wiped away my dreams. Just remembering everything I went through to write this book, I cannot believe I survived it all.

I also lost both of my father's parents during this period, which was very painful, because I loved them very much. They had both been deteriorating for years, since my grandfather had his stroke after the 2008 war, and they had been bedridden for a long time, lying side by side while my father and the nurses we hired took turns taking care of them. Then one day in May 2014, my grandmother suddenly called out my grandfather's name. She said, "I think that I'm moving to another world. Remember that I love you." Then she died. After that, my grandfather said he had nothing left to do on earth. He had turned to God after his stroke—he was raised as a Communist and had no interest in religion before, but my grandmother had always been a person of faith, and he joined her in that faith during those last years. He spent a lot of time praying, and even spoke to the pope before he died that November, six months after my grandmother. He couldn't stay away from her that long—she had been his true love since kindergarten.

Working in Tbilisi, my father still managed to travel to visit his parents during those last years. He then found work as a psychiatrist again, treating the victims of the addiction epidemic that claimed my ex-husband and so many others from our generation. He took a job at a hospital in the western part of Georgia because the pay was better there—so he'd had to leave my mother again. After all those years living in Russia, he was used to this kind of arrangement and has been living and working there for four years as I write this. My mother says he's used to being alone, but she still worries he doesn't have anyone to look after him. Luckily, my father was never one of those typical Georgian men who yelled at their wives for not having dinner on the table on time. More often than not, when my father lived with us, he was the one who made dinner, since my mother was usually working.

My mother and father talk every day, and he tries to travel back to Tbilisi twice a week, although the distance is long, and as he gets older, the trip gets harder to make. My mother also tries to visit him as much as possible, and they travel together whenever they can with my daughter, which is their favorite thing to do. That's part of the reason I finance the trips, because it also gives my parents, who sacrificed so much for me, an opportunity to spend time together and enjoy life.

Like that of my grandparents, my parents' story is another great love story. You can see it in the way they treat each other, and have always treated each other, even through the hardest times. They may not have enough income to give each other everything they want, but they are always there for each other. They always wait for each other's opinion. They never make a decision without the other. They have divided their duties so that they are together even when they are not, because everything they do is integrated, not separated. I hope that someday, I can find a partner who treats me with the same kind of love and respect. Then again, I may have found that person already, but we will get to that a little later ...

At that point, during my first years of freedom, the only love story that mattered to me was the one between my child and me. I was determined that her childhood would be as happy and fulfilling as possible, so I made sure her schedule was full each and every day, starting from kindergarten. Whenever she expressed an interest in something, I would find a class where she could explore that thing, whether it was singing or dancing or art or science or a sport or one of dozens of other things she tried. When she lost interest in something, I did not push her to continue pursuing an activity she no longer loved; instead, I saw it as a door opening—an opportunity for her to explore something new.

We attended every exhibition of arts—theater, movies, even the opera, which she became fascinated with at the age of six after sitting all the way through a three-hour performance. She had her own opinion about everything—she watched ballet and could speak for hours about what she liked here and what she didn't like there. Over time, she developed a strong sense of what her talents are, what matters to her and how she likes to spend her time. Her biggest passion is science. We used to do different experiments at home—we had an ant farm when she was in kindergarten, and she would bring insects home and observe their behavior as they built colonies and carried food back and forth. She took notes in a little notebook, like a real scientist. I brought home Triops, a species of crustacean eggs dating back 220 million years, and we observed them through a microscope and watched them hatch, popping out of their eggs, and she took notes on that too. Animals were and still are her biggest passion, so we had, at various times, a snake, rabbits, hamsters, pet rats, parrots, an ocelot, and a chameleon, plus all the various worms and insects we needed to feed them. We also have two cats. We have adopted so many different animals that our apartment is like our own private zoo.

When I had time off, my daughter and I would travel together. I loved to take her hiking all around Georgia, exploring the seashore and the ancient fortresses that are hidden in the mountains. When she would get tired, instead of turning back, I would put her up on my shoulders and keep going until we reached our destination. I wanted to teach her not to give up on her goals, whether they were small ones or big ones. But what I really wanted was to give my daughter the whole universe, to show her how beautiful our world is, whether we were able to be together or not, whether things were easy or hard. As a single mom with a demanding job, I could never spend as much time as I wanted to with my child. So I focused on the quality of the time we spent together. I knew I could not always be there for everything, but I could make sure the time we did spend together made her feel safe and loved and at home in the world.

Plus, all that focus on my daughter made it easier not to think too much about myself. Honestly, I was too busy to think, period. I woke up at six in the morning every day to clean up the apartment, do laundry, make breakfast, and make dinner for myself and Sandra's babysitter for when I got home. Sometimes I would make a bunch of dinners at once, so I would have them ready when I needed them. I left for work at nine in the morning and sometimes worked until late at night, which meant my mother or grandmother would need to watch Sandra after the babysitter went home. I would be so busy at work during the day that I couldn't call the babysitter to find out how Sandra was doing, so we would communicate by sending each other messages. Sometimes I didn't even have time to go to the toilet—I trained myself to resist the urge for up to ten hours (which can be a useful skill at times, like long airplane flights). I was kind of like a robot who was programmed to get everything done in the shortest possible amount of time before moving on to the next task.

But still … after a while, I realized I felt different. First, I caught myself smiling more often than I did before. Then I noticed that inner feeling of anxiety that used to follow me everywhere I went, which I thought was just a natural part of my personality, had disappeared. I had never been able to go out in the street without worrying about being chased or someone pulling a knife on me before. I had never been able to look at my messages without wondering what insults or threats I would have to read. Now I could. I could sleep through the night without waking up at every little noise or being tormented by nightmares. I still only slept three or four hours a night, but I actually slept during those hours, more deeply and peacefully than I could ever remember, every single night.

For the first time, I was experiencing serenity. And that serenity gave me space to finally think about myself.

I had never been the kind of woman who went out for manicures or pedicures, or had facial treatments or massages at the spa. I did not even buy clothes for myself beyond the necessary things, and not only because my ex-husband had emptied my bank account. I had never really cared about those things. I thought it was all a waste of time, but maybe that was only because I had real, major problems in my life that I was constantly trying to solve. Now that they were behind me, I started thinking about myself differently. And when I changed my attitude toward myself, I noticed other people started to treat me differently. I was no longer "poor Tamar," the girl with the crazy, drug-addicted husband; I was a successful businesswoman with her whole life ahead of her. That was the moment when I started to think not just about survival, but also about my future.

***

Most of that future was focused on building CBS Group. The merger that I had been working on, which my ex had tried to sabotage, went through, and the deal was successful. We wanted to get involved in more big, transformative projects like that—projects that would build Georgia's infrastructure and economy. However, in order to build these new things or clean up and get the most out of the assets we owned, there was a constant need for cash. I did a lot of analysis, deciding which companies to divest, looking for the assets that could be capitalized the most, the ones that might not be as profitable in our portfolio in the future. I started small, with maybe a $6 million transaction, but continued to build, ultimately facilitating transactions of hundreds of millions of dollars. We were able to divest from the companies that were draining money out of the company, and I was able to build up the cash cows, invest the money they generated, and build the portfolio we have now. CBS Group's company mission is "to grow the future together," and that is exactly what we are doing.

I got involved not only in local negotiations, but also international negotiations with different groups, having headquarters in almost every part of the world. I traveled a lot. Many international companies were interested in doing transactions with us, along with international consulting firms and governmental sectors of neighboring countries like Russia, Azerbaijan, Armenia, and even Kazakhstan. We began to have an impact not only in our own country, but also all across the region.

The change we're helping create in Georgia isn't just about building a modern, functional infrastructure; it's about doing business in a new way that's more aligned with Europe and the West. For example, through our minibus contract, CBS Group has transformed Georgians' attitudes around how things should be paid for. The minibus turned out to be a perfect case study for making this change, because minibuses, called marshrutka, have long been the most popular form of transport in Tbilisi and in cities all over our part of the world. They were especially important after the Soviet Union collapsed and the government-run transport systems fell apart.

Since that time, most of the minibuses had been privately owned and operated on the black market. They were completely unregulated, with different criminal gangs controlling the different lines so that none of them worked together in any logical way. The buses themselves were old and not well maintained, so there were frequent breakdowns and safety issues. And of course, not a penny was paid to the government treasury to keep up the roads (which were a mess), or impose regulations to protect passengers, or standardize the fares and transport lines, or do anything to make transport better and more reliable.

The City of Tbilisi decided to change that. They held a contest to find a company to take over, transform, and operate the transport system in an orderly, regulated way. A group of companies owned by our shareholder won the contract, which gave CBS Group the license to transport people within the capital. But first, we had to transform our broken minibus system into something new and functional.

Our goal was to create the same kind of system you'd find in a European country—a systemized, regulated transport system that was safe and reliable and took people where they needed to go. And in order to make sure we collected standardized fees and paid taxes, we also designed an innovative new system of payment, where every fare could be paid by card, automatically tracked, and accounted for. Using the government's Metromoney cards, for example, riders could then purchase and top up at metro stations or pay by debit card from the bank. This was part of Georgia's shift from a primarily cash-based economy dominated by the black market to one where most payments are made by card. In Tbilisi, 100 percent of the payments for municipal transportation and minibuses take place via card payments; I'd estimate that with the same system active throughout Georgia, logic would indicate the distribution of the population's cash transactions in public transportation to be no more than 25 percent. In this way, everything is transparent, paid by credit cards or transportation cards. This has changed our country, as well as the perception of consumers in Georgia, in a very meaningful way, bringing trust and stability. I'm so proud to be a part of that shift. It is part of what I dreamed of when I was planning my future as a student in the Italian school.

Another part of my dream—to get my MBA at a European school—has also come true. In 2017, I was accepted into a very prestigious MBA program operated through a partnership between my alma mater, the Caucasus School of Business, and Grenoble, the famous French school of management. They offered a two-year program that enabled me to work in Georgia and only travel occasionally for my studies. It was a very tough period, having a full-time job, studying for my MBA, and being a single mom, trying to connect the financial dots in order to survive. I am so grateful to CBS, which financed my studies, but even with its help, it was still a crazy time.

The program was structured so that every month, the professors and lecturers from Grenoble would come to Georgia and deliver an entire month's worth of instruction in a five-day period. We would be in class from morning until night for those five days, and then I would go back to my regular job as a CFO. It was hell but a very familiar kind of hell for me—not all that different from when I was finishing the Italian school while prepping for my university entrance exam, or when I was working at the Bank of Georgia while going to school and taking care of my husband in prison. Besides, it wasn't all bad. Part of this "hell" involved occasional trips to the Grenoble campus in France, and nobody would call France hell! I remember so well taking trips around France and its neighboring countries with my MBA friends. It was like a first breath of air by a newborn, when your lungs still ache and hurt but you can breathe independently!

In 2019, when I was thirty-two, I learned I would be graduating with distinction from Grenoble. I planned to travel to France with my mother and my daughter to receive my diploma, then take a celebration trip through Bavaria and Vienna. But as the day drew closer, there was a complication. Five years before, in 2014, my grandmother had been diagnosed with blood cancer. Since she lived with my mother, who is a doctor, she outlived her prognosis by several years, remaining very active and involved in every family decision. But by the end of my MBA studies, she was confined to bed and could not move, let alone make the trip to France to see me graduate. Still, she insisted that my mother should go. Seeing me get my MBA had been my mother's dream, and now that it was finally happening after everything I went through, after my ex-husband almost destroyed that dream, my grandmother thought nothing should stop her from seeing it finally come true. So my mother agreed to travel to France with Sandra and me, and they both were there to see me receive my diploma and graduate with distinction.

The next day, we flew to Munich to begin our tour of Bavaria, and I received a message that my grandmother had died. I urgently changed our tickets back to Georgia, and that same evening, we came back to say goodbye to her. I know that she was proud of me.

Chapter 12

FACING THE FUTURE

In the middle of writing this book, I was given an incredible opportunity. In recognition of the demands, pressure, and hard work involved in being a C-suite leader of one of the biggest holdings in Georgia, we sometimes have the opportunity to attend programs in magnificent locations like the Swiss Alps—to ski, yes, but also to enjoy the chance for continuous learning while continuing to realize the bank's mission. On such an occasion, I was able to travel to Germany to watch Georgia compete in the Euro competition in football. It was so gratifying to be a part of history—this was the first time Georgia was included in the tournament since the Soviet Union collapsed. Having a presence there was a great leap for our country, because now all of Europe knew about us. It was another small step toward taking our place in the Western world, and I felt so good to be part of it.

I had only been home for a day or so when our founder called me and asked me to represent CBS Group at an investment summit organized by the US government. The US Embassy in Georgia had been working to organize a group to travel to Washington, DC, and while CBS had not initially been included and registration was closed, they realized the oversight and sent a last-minute invitation. I had two days to get my documents in order and go through all the security checks and interviews with the consulate. We had to book our flight the day before we knew that we were approved. It all happened within hours. Before I knew it, I was on a plane to the United States.

In a way, my life today looks a lot like the life I thought I would build when I was on that first flight to Italy when I was a girl, flooded with an enormous sense of possibility and of being a part of something greater. I am a part of the international business community, representing Georgia on the global stage, having traveled all over the former Soviet Union and to places as far away as Japan for my work.

Just like I dreamed as a girl, today I am part of the generation that is shaping Georgia's post-Soviet economy, helping to build a stronger, fairer, more modern society. I had a real full-circle moment recently when the Bank of Georgia, the company that trained me and launched my career, invited me to come back and train their bankers and corporate credit analysts through a program structured by Alte University. This is new for me—I'm not a professor, I've never taught a class, I didn't have a set program to use, and I've never studied to be a trainer. But when the positive feedback came in, the university then asked me to design a program for different banks, covering all sorts of issues like copyright training. In addition to that, I have been invited to teach a class at a business school, working with young people just like I once was. I'm excited to share my knowledge so they can continue to shape our economy as our nation evolves. They will continue to build a stronger Georgia, where more is becoming possible every day.

Yet my country still faces challenges. Because of our location and our history, we continue to be pulled back and forth between Russia and Europe, between two different views of government and authority, between conflict and peace. My hope is that, regardless of what political viewpoints prevail, we will continue to move forward and build a country that offers equal opportunity and freedom to everyone. No matter what happens, I know that I will keep working toward building that future, for my daughter and for my country.

***

Working for CBS Group has put me on the front lines of building this new Georgia. We have been involved in developing and building some of the most significant improvements to the region, including the submarine internet cable from Georgia to Bulgaria that I mentioned earlier. The negotiations for the license were intense—all the countries in the Black Sea basin were involved, including Turkey, Russia, Bulgaria, and Romania, and they all had to give us the right to build in their territories. We also had to negotiate with the two or three suppliers in the world that provide the submarines and big technical ships needed for a project of that scope. Today, because of those successful negotiations, Georgia is able to have the only direct connection between the Western world and the Eastern world.

Another important project was making Tbilisi's natural gas pipeline safer and more reliable. The company's owners had been outside of Georgia, and they failed to invest in the pipeline, leaving it so unsafe you never knew when you would have gas or when you would not, and which area of the city might explode like fireworks because of a gas leak. Since CBS Group acquired the holding and invested in bringing it up to modern standards, there have not been any of these events. Gas delivery has been safer and more consistent.

These sorts of changes have had a huge impact on the country, making our society feel more stable and safer, and our company has actually received some of the credit for these changes. Georgians know the name CBS Group. They know we are a responsible company that is working to provide and improve the services that will make our country stronger. Trust in us is so high that, when the COVID-19 pandemic happened, instead of calling the help lines set up by the government, people called our call center, looking for solutions to their problems. As one of the three original employees of CBS Group, I can't tell you how proud I am to have helped create a business that has earned that level of trust.

Right now, we are breaking up a monopoly of our mobile system. We were able to buy a mobile company from Russian investors. We are now building a company that will not only increase competitiveness but also bring Georgia in line with regulations between our country and Europe, focusing on the fairness and competitiveness of the markets for customers.

We have come a long way since 2013, when we started with three employees and a single shareholder with a bunch of scattered holdings and a dream of putting them to good use. Back then, we had a total of only one hundred or two hundred employees across all our businesses. Today we have more than eight thousand employees and are growing at a 10 percent annual rate. In such a small country, we are contributing a huge percentage of the GDP. In the beginning, all our assets were scattered, and no one took us seriously when we would apply for a loan. Now the banks are chasing us. And we're only just getting started.

***

As for me, there have been big changes in my life as well—both professional and personal, as I alluded to earlier ...

Back in 2012, when I was still working for the Bank of Georgia, I'd had the opportunity to work on a very important project in terms of rebuilding my country—the "internetization" of Georgia. We financed the project, which included bringing all of Georgia's schools and police stations online, putting fiber optics everywhere, and bringing consistent, high-quality internet to every village in the country. I was the manager on this account, which was a very capital-intensive project, so for a while, I went to my client's offices almost every day to collect information and interview the founders, as well as their new CFO and his chief financial analyst, to understand their strategy.

This new chief financial analyst was young and handsome, and (while I did not know this at the time) he was attracted to me. As we were working together, he did some research to find out who I was—and once he learned that I was married, and that my husband was a criminal and a crazy person, he decided not to pursue me. Knowing my ex-husband, this was probably a wise decision on his part.

Years later, when I was at CBS Group, I was involved in negotiations to acquire that telecommunications company. We were starting the acquisition in the summer after wrapping up another big project, so before the first meeting, I took five days off and went to the Black Sea with Alexsandra for a vacation. I came back to work tanned and relaxed and happy, and it must have shown. I walked into our meeting with all the executives and the consultants from one of the Big Four audit companies, and there was my old colleague, who was now the CFO of the company we were trying to acquire. He later said he "lost his ability to talk" when I walked in. All the feelings he had for me five years before came rushing back.

This time, he decided to pursue me, although at first, I did not realize this was his plan. We would be working hard doing due diligence, and he would slip in personal questions like, What's your marital status? Did you leave your husband again? Are you seeing anyone else?

If I was ever going to date another man, this one was a good prospect. He went to the same university I did (though he's two years younger, he was three years behind me because of the school age cutoff). He was very successful. Unlike me, he actually did make it to Georgia State University in the United States, earning his bachelor's degree and becoming the first student from Georgia to start his own business in the United States. In his younger days, he was a self-taught programmer, able even to detect bugs in the governmental sector's systems. He was still a teenager when he was offered a position in the IT department of the parliament of Georgia. He was smart, educated, and good-looking, but more importantly, he seemed like a truly, genuinely nice person. However, I did not want anything more than friendship from this man, or any man. I had been in love before, and it almost killed me.

Our negotiations hit a roadblock when our rival in the acquisition offered a higher price beyond what I was prepared to pay, because it was above the market value. But the CFO and I continued our friendship, growing closer but still never crossing that line. Then in 2018, my health problems caught up with me. I was in the middle of working toward my MBA, and I wasn't just burning the candle at both ends—I was burning the whole candle. Between my job, school, and motherhood, I had been pushing myself even harder than usual. Of course, I didn't pay any attention to my health, because who had time to think about health? But that's the thing about the human body—if you ignore it for too long, it will make you pay attention. And mine did.

Everything hit me at once. The heart palpitations and vision trouble and shaking from my autoimmune disease came back. My hormonal problems came back. I was a complete mess. How was I ever going to get everything done?

That's when this man, my friend, the CFO, showed me what kind of person he is. He stepped in and helped me get through this period, even helping me take care of my daughter. And in return, he asked for nothing. It did not matter if I didn't want to marry him; he told me that he would be by my side, whatever happened.

No man had ever said anything like that to me—or if my ex-husband ever did, it would have been a lie to get me to do something he wanted. It had been four or five years since my ex went to jail, and for all of those years, I had been alone. I had rebuilt the wall around my heart even higher and stronger than it had been the first time.

And suddenly this man appeared in my life like an angel—like a life preserver in the middle of the dark, empty sea that was my heart. After all the disappointment and all the things that I had gone through, the fact that a man was offering me help, for nothing, was almost beyond my comprehension.

Helping me meant he spent a lot of time with Sandra. He loves children, and she fell in love with him. However, there may have been more to their connection than his fondness for children—I think he understood that the way to my heart goes through my daughter's heart, and if Sandra did not accept him, I would not have started a relationship with him. But she did more than accept him—she advocated for him. She told me she wanted a father like him, that she wanted a little sister or little brother, that she wanted me to build a family with this man. She forced me to think about what a healthy relationship might look like, and to admit to myself that maybe it was time for me to finally try to have one.

So for the second time in my life, I agreed to date. And shockingly, he didn't do anything terrible to me. He didn't yell or scream or threaten. He didn't care who I talked to, and he didn't ask me for anything except my companionship.

When the COVID-19 pandemic happened, Georgia went on lockdown, and like people in most of the country, I started working from home. My boyfriend was one of the few people who was allowed to go out to work, because he had taken a position as a CFO of one of the biggest cable producers in Georgia, and his work was considered an "essential service." After work, he would come by our apartment to visit Sandra and me. And sometimes, he would stay so long that he would forget to leave before curfew … so he would spend the night at our house. It started happening more and more often.

The pandemic was a difficult, lonely time for a lot of people, but for me, it was almost like a vacation. For the first time, I was able to spend all day, every day with my daughter, and sometimes at night, we were joined by my very nice boyfriend, who treated us like princesses. The three of us grew closer, and it wasn't long before we made a decision to have a child together.

There were several reasons for this, all well thought out. My doctors had warned me that because of my health problems, if I did not have a baby soon, it might be impossible, and then Sandra would never have a brother or sister. The pandemic presented the perfect opportunity for me to have a baby—depending on how long we were locked down, I might be able to spend my whole pregnancy working from home, which would be easier on my health, and spend those first weeks and maybe even months at home with my newborn. My boyfriend reminded me that he did not care if I married him, or even promised to only be with him for the rest of my life. He said he would be the happiest man in the world if he could have his first child with me, the woman he loved. So we did it.

I got pregnant, and it was a good thing we did it during lockdown, because my pregnancy was even more difficult than it was with Sandra. My autoimmune disease treated the baby like a cancer or an alien invasion, fighting the pregnancy and trying to push it out. I almost lost my baby two or three times, and each time, my boyfriend was there by my side all night long, sitting by my bed, getting whatever permission we needed to go to the hospital if we had to. Of course I was still working and managed to close two very complex trans-actions—an important contract in the transportation sector and the acquisition of an electricity distribution company—in between helping my daughter navigate online school, cooking with one hand and holding a laptop with the other, doing all the chores, and sleeping three to four hours a night. It was a crazy time, but it was also such a happy time. My daughter and I got all the quality time together we had missed over the years, all in those few months. We had so much fun, singing and drawing and inventing games. We didn't need the rest of the world when we had each other.

The transportation deal was so big and so complicated that the process lasted past the birth of my son, whom I named Ioane, the Georgian version of "John," after John the Baptist. I had an online meeting on the project from my hospital room, four hours after my son was born via natural childbirth—I didn't get the pain medication because I heard that makes labor last longer, and I needed to get it over with so I could have my meeting! Before the lockdown period was over, I managed to conclude this deal involving city hall, the banks, and our company, which is now one of the important assets in CBS Group's portfolio.

The lockdown really transformed me from a financial manager to a crisis manager—both of those transactions happened because I was able to pivot and get the most out of the situation we were in. Since everything was devalued during this period, I saw it as a good time to make acquisitions, knowing we would be in an even stronger position when the economy rebounded. Georgia handled the COVID-19 pandemic very well, especially in the beginning, compared to the other nations in Europe. The government communicated in a very clear manner, they imposed strict regulations quickly, and our health-care system operated at a very high level, with enough space in our hospitals to handle the sick population and with plenty of doctors to treat them. Still, the pandemic was a huge crisis across the globe, and we suffered economically like everyone else.

This gave CBS Group another opportunity to show our commitment to our country. Our founder insisted that, no matter how hard it was on our margins, we were going to keep all the employees of all our holdings, whether they were coming to work or not. We continued paying the salaries of everyone who was employed before the lockdown, which not only kept them fed and housed, but also contributed to the overall stability of Georgia's economy. We demonstrated social responsibility toward our country. That's how I see and how I respect the company I'm working for. I'm proud to have come through the pandemic without even laying one person off, unlike so many other companies in Georgia and around the world. There were about seven thousand people working for CBS Group or one of our holdings before the pandemic. Today, we are more than eight thousand employees strong.

***

My baby Ioane is the sunshine in my life. He was not an easy baby. He didn't sleep through the night for a year and three months, so neither did I. But he got past that, and he is growing into an amazing boy. I try to grasp every moment I have with him. He's so sweet, sharing his warmth and love with everyone, but at the same time, he knows what he wants, how he wants to be, and how to put everything in its place. And of course, he adores his father.

Still, even though the father of my son is an extraordinarily nice person, and responsible, and not in any way a criminal, I have still not decided to have a "normal" family. Because, honestly, I'm still afraid. I'm still struggling to trust in men, and right now, I feel more comfortable living separately, being friends, without a legal commitment or even a commitment to share a home. He's the perfect father and the perfect friend to me, and I feel so lucky to finally have such a good person in my life, who appreciates me and wants me to be happy, and wants me to do what I want to do, as opposed to what he wants me to do. But I am not yet ready to tear down my walls a second time. I feel most comfortable keeping things this way, living a separate life from the father of my child, even though I love him and think of him as family. It is just easier for me, and because he is such a good person, he supports me in every way he can. He still tells me that even if I don't decide to live with him, even if I eventually choose another man, he will still be the man who will always wait for me and will always fight for me.

I am so grateful to have him in my life.

***

As for the story of my ex, of course he continued to call me from jail, even after I sent him there for his crimes against me. He begged me to set him free, promising that he would never, ever bother me again.

I communicated with him from time to time—sometimes I answered his calls and letters; sometimes I didn't. I was always trying to find that "golden middle," knowing that someday he would get out of jail, and when he did, I did not want to face his aggression again.

Luckily for me, the prison system in Georgia has changed a lot since he went to jail the first time, back when we were newlyweds. Instead of easy access to drugs, he received drug treatment, as well as the counseling and mental health treatment he had clearly needed throughout his life. And after approximately three and a half years, he was clean and sober and in a better place than he had been in all the years I had known him. So I talked with the prosecutors and agreed to give my consent to let him out, with the understanding that he would never, ever appear in our lives again. And amazingly, he stuck to the agreement. He came out of jail, and there were no threats or surprise visits. There was only a letter, asking for money to help my ex-husband move from Georgia to the United States. I replied that I was not going to help him anymore. He was on his own.

I did not wish to know anything about him and his life after prison, but he always found a way to remind me about his existence anyway. Soon after he came out of jail, a woman showed up at my door, telling me my ex-husband was still in love with me and begging me to "let him go." I said, "You poor girl, you have no idea what this man is really like." I still don't know whether that was the same girl who had sent me threatening emails and called me. But regardless, I gave the same advice: get as far away from him as possible, like I did.

Somehow, my ex-husband made it to the United States. I still hear from him periodically—he writes to me and messages me to tell me that I am still the special one for him, that he is a different person now, that he wants to be a father to his daughter. Sandra wants nothing to do with him—she has asked for permission to change her surname to mine, to sever that last tie to her father and his family. I have not let her do that. I told her that when she turns eighteen, if she still wants to change her name, she should be the one to do it, not me. Because her name is also her heritage, and I believe she should be proud of that heritage, because it belongs to her and nobody else. It proves that she, like her mother, is a survivor.

***

Right now, my life is as calm as it has ever been. Sometimes I feel like it's the calm before the storm. But maybe the storm will not be a bad one. Maybe the storm will be a storm of change.

Georgia is also facing a storm right now. We came through the COVID-19 pandemic very well—the economy was growing by double digits, inflation was at targeted levels, and the relationships between our neighbors had stabilized. We were on track for admission to the European Union. But in Georgia, instability is our stability. Russia invaded Ukraine and threw our region back into turmoil, and now everyone is wondering what will happen next. I'm not a politician; I'm a businessperson and a finance professional. But I know that political turmoil, no matter who is responsible, is never good for business. It hurts people on both sides. So my hope, as always, is for stability, peace, and freedom for everyone to pursue their dreams. I hope to avoid another blitz that washes everything away.

Still, whatever happens, just like so many times before, we Georgians will try to manage, and we'll try to survive. We already know how to navigate through tough circumstances, because in the end, it is always the same game. Georgia is always at the crossroads, always on the edge, between East and West, freedom and repression, war and peace. If you look at my tiny country and at me, a young woman struggling to make it in that tiny country, you might think neither of us should still be alive.

But still, we are here. And we are ready to shape our future.

Acknowledgments

As I sit here trying to encapsulate the vast ocean of gratitude that fills my heart, I am overwhelmed by the countless ways you, my friends, have shaped my life. This book is not just a testament to my journey; it is a celebration of the love and support you've shown me, without which this story could never have been told.

Whether from my childhood, university, CBS, Grenoble, the bank, or my clients—my friends make me the luckiest person to get to keep their company. They are my most precious assets. I once thought that only childhood friends can really be sincere, honest, and loyal, but I was gravely mistaken.

Soulmate Natia M., you have been my guiding star, always there to illuminate my darkest hours. When I got the opportunity of writing this autobiography, you were the one who assured me that my story was worth telling. Your unshakeable faith in me, your willingness to listen to my endless drafts, and your thoughtful insights have been invaluable. I remember the late-night talks, where your wisdom and gentle encouragement would lift my spirits and renew my determination. Thank you for being my anchor and for believing in me even when I struggled to believe in myself, you've been my companion in every sense of the word.

Gvantsa G., our journey together has been a symphony of laughter, adventure, and poignant moments. From the spontaneous road trips to our deep, soul-baring conversations that stretched into the early hours of the morning, you were the source of inspiration when I needed it most. I vividly recall the day when everything seemed to crumble around me, and you showed up at my doorstep with a smile, chocolate, and ice-cream, and a promise that we would get through it together.

My beautiful Tamar M., your words have a way of settling in my heart, and your friendship has been a guiding force that I treasure deeply. You are like a butterfly, which reminds me to savor the little moments and find happiness amidst chaos. That's why I am grateful to have you as a godmother to my daughter.

Ana J., your endless optimism and infectious joy have been a beacon of light in my life. I am eternally grateful for you standing by my side through every twist and turn, even though you had your own troubles to overcome.

Tamar J., you have this incredible gift of turning the most challenging situations into opportunities for growth, and your perspective has been a cornerstone of my personal and creative journey. I recall one particular night, sitting in the bank, when you imparted wisdom that changed my outlook on life.

Eka K., you have been my truth-teller, my confidant, my sounding board since childhood. Your ability to speak with honesty and love has provided me with clarity in times of confusion and heartache. Even though we do not see each other often, I know you are always there for me.

Natia T., your kindness and unwavering support have been a sanctuary for me. When I faced crossroads, uncertain of the path to take, your wise counsel guided me. The memories of our university days are etched in my heart.

Ana T., you have always been a symbol of a strong woman and a brilliant mother for me. Thank you for the unconditional love shared.

Magda M., in the moments when I felt lost and desolate, desperate in my abilities to be able to get my MBA, your gentle presence was a reminder of the love that surrounds me. You have this innate ability to make everyone feel seen, heard, and valued.

Nana Ch., your empathy and understanding have helped me navigate through some of the most difficult chapters of my life. We swam together through the years of school and university. Thank you for your quiet strength and for always being a source of comfort and unwavering support.

Zura Kh., your words were few but emotions ran deep. Your companionship is my greatest blessing. Your and your wife's love fuels my spirit.

David K., your wise counsel and your genuine kindness have influenced my life in ways I cannot adequately express. You have an incredible ability to lift people's spirits. It is your voice that echoes in my mind when I write.

Nestan M. and Misha N., your stories inspire my own. Your exemplary love and support have warmed my heart many times, enabling my hopes and feelings reborn from ashes.

Friend whom I call sister, special friends, to whom I have been a bridesmaid or to whose child I have been a godmother, or vice versa, my new friends from the travel adventures, whole CBS group, and friends, both mentioned here and those whose names are etched in my heart, your presence has been the tapestry of my life.

You, my friends, my chosen family have been my pillars, my mirrors, my stars guiding me through the darkest nights, beautiful planets whom I am so lucky to be in orbit with.

I remain thankful for my life which made me stronger; I have a beautiful daughter. I have gained more than I have lost. This book is, and always will be, a testament to the power of friendship, love, and the ability to remain a human who acts humane in every aspect of life.

With all my love and deepest gratitude,
Tamar

About the Author

Tamar Gakharia was born and raised in the heart of Tbilisi, Georgia, where the foundations of passion, resilience, and a relentless curiosity for life were nurtured from a young age. Growing up amidst the vibrant tapestry of Tbilisi, Tamar discovered early on the power of dreams and the strength of the human spirit.

Life has been a journey of remarkable experiences for Tamar, one characterized by both tremendous highs and formidable lows. While pursuing her studies in business school of Caucasus University, Tamar set out to explore her professional landscape, immersing herself in the banking industry. Each role taken on in one of the leading banks in her country, each challenge faced, has been a stepping stone toward greater understanding and growth, which led her to the position of the CFO at CBS Group LLC, one of the biggest business holdings in Georgia. While trailing her career as a C-level manager, Tamar earned her MBA degree both from her alma mater and Grenoble Ecole de Management, specializing in innovations management and finance, respectively.

Throughout her career, Tamar has held steadfast to the principles of justice, innovation, and progress, not just as a professional but as a passion that drives each endeavor. Her work has earned recognition, but more meaningful than any award has been the impact made on lives touched along the way.

What truly sets Tamar apart is a deep, abiding love for the simple and beautiful moments of life. An avid hiker, she finds joy in traveling, believing that it's these moments that fill our lives with richness and meaning.

Family has always been the cornerstone of Tamar's world. Currently residing in Tbilisi, Georgia, with two beautiful children, every day is cherished as a reminder of what truly matters. It's this sense of connection and love that has fueled the stories shared in this book.

This autobiography is more than a recounting of events; it is a heartfelt narrative filled with the laughter, tears, struggles, and triumphs that define Tamar's journey. Through these pages, she invites readers to walk a mile in her shoes, to feel the pulse of dreams pursued and lessons learned.

To all who read this, know that you too have stories worth telling, journeys worth taking. And in every step of your own path, may you find the same strength, hope, and inspiration that Tamar has found in her odyssey.

Connect with Tamar on Facebook or LinkedIn to share your stories and continue this beautiful journey of connection and shared hummanity.

www.ingramcontent.com/pod-product-compliance
Lightning Source LLC
Chambersburg PA
CBHW020455100426
42813CB00031B/3371/J